Outdoor Education

in Girl Scouting

Girl Scouts of the U.S.A.

420 Fifth Avenue

New York, N.Y. 10018-2798

GIRL SCOUTS OF THE U.S.A.®

B. LaRae Orullian, *President*

Mary Rose Main, *National Executive Director*

Inquiries regarding this book should be addressed to

Membership and Program Cluster, Girl Scouts of the U.S.A.,

420 Fifth Avenue, New York, N.Y. 10018-2798.

Author:

Carolyn L. Kennedy

Contributors:

María L. Cabán

Joan W. Fincutter

Sharon Woods Hussey

Harriet S. Mosatche

Donna L. Nye

First Impression 1996

Printed in the United States of America

ISBN 0-88441-488-4

Photographers:

Nansi Bauman: Page 17. **Tom Bernard:** Page 64. **Teri Cluck:** Pages 31, 62, 101. **Photodisc, Inc.:** Cover, pages 3, 9, 22, 26, 29, 40, 92, 94, 97, 123, 164. **GSUSA photo library:** Pages 5, 8, 15, 28, 33, 59, 60, 77, 79, 83, 114, 117, 120, 127, 137, 140, 142, 149, 153, 154, 158, 163, 165. **Ed Haas:** Pages 24, 25, 32, 33, 37, 41, 42, 43, 44, 45, 46, 47, 48, 49, 50, 53, 54, 55, 56, 57, 70, 72, 75, 81, 86, 87, 90, 95, 96, 102, 103, 109, 111, 115, 119, 124, 126, 127, 128, 133, 151, 152, 156, 160, 162. **Elizabeth Hathon:** Page 38. **Ameen Howrani:** Page 7. **Jack Jones:** Page 139. **Carolyn Kennedy:** Pages 21, 35, 36, 123, 128, 133, 141, 146, 147. **National Oceanic & Atmospheric Administration:** Page 98. **National Science Partnership for Girl Scouts and Science Museums:** From *Weather Watch* video. Page 131. **River Bluffs Girl Scout Council:** Page 61.

Contents

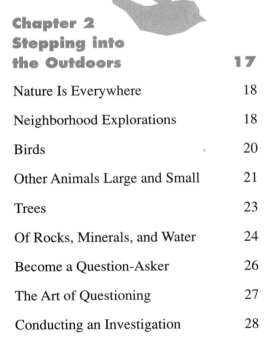

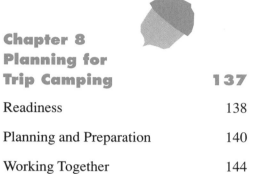

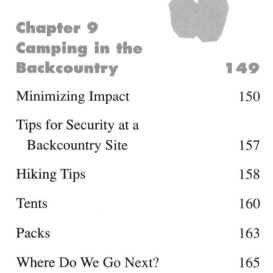

Chapter 1

Introduction

Each year millions of people around the globe enjoy outdoor recreational activities in their leisure time. These activities are an important part of life—a time for personal reflection, for challenge, for being together with family and friends, or being alone with a beautiful sunset. Many young people learn their respect for the outdoors through organized activities such as those provided by Girl Scouting. Under the guidance of a trained and enthusiastic adult leader, girls may take their first hike and, through a series of activities, gain the skill to plan trips on their own to destinations of their choosing. The information in this book leads us out the door to explore our planet and enjoy and care for its resources.

This book is written to help Girl Scout leaders prepare themselves and the girls with whom they work to enjoy outdoor experiences together. It is to be used along with the age-level handbook and leaders' guide, Safety-Wise, *and training provided by the local Girl Scout council.*

Girls can experience the outdoors in many ways. One group might decide to take an afternoon walk to a local park. Hiking through a state forest might be right for another. Some girls may never want to sleep outside but may enjoy working in a community garden. Others may enjoy a strenuous outdoor activity like playing soccer or bicycling that allows them to return home at night. The goal is to allow each girl opportunities to explore and develop an understanding of the outdoors and find a comfortable relationship that works for her.

A New Perspective

Space-age fabrics, foods, and lightweight metals, all produced at relatively low cost, have revolutionized the types of clothing and equipment available for outdoor recreation in recent years. New activities are constantly being invented. At the same time, open space near population centers is being consumed by development. With increasing numbers of people using parks and outdoor spaces, we must look at our outdoor pursuits with new insight. Our activities must touch the Earth lightly, leaving as few traces of our presence as possible. The new challenge is to learn how our recreational activities can affect the earth and learn how to change, reduce, or eliminate those that pollute, erode, or damage the environment.

Focusing on Girls

Outdoor education occurs when Girl Scout program activities are held outdoors. Outdoor activities provide opportunities for each girl to grow as an individual. The most important outcomes are changes in how she feels about herself, relates to others, develops values, and contributes to her community. It is the girl's ability to feel good about herself and her contribution to the success of the group that are important, not her ability to name twenty birds or tie ten kinds of knots.

In Girl Scouting, outdoor education is defined as the effective utilization of Girl Scout program in the outdoor setting enabling girls to grow in each of the areas of the four Girl Scout program goals. The primary approach is experiential learning through which girls develop their outdoor recreational interests and skills.

Progression in Outdoor Activities

As you, the leader, discuss with girls the activities they wish to plan for the future, you may find girls who have no interest in outdoor pursuits and girls who just can't wait for the next outdoor activity. For girls with little outdoor experience, start with activities in the most familiar outdoor environment before venturing far from home. Girl Scout program is built on the concept of progression—acquiring the skills needed to progress to more difficult or highly skilled activities. As girls build their confidence, progressive outdoor experiences can be planned farther and farther away from home or using more complex skills. The chart on pages 10-13 shows many of the progressive activities available in Girl Scouting.

Outdoor education activities can help meet the needs of today's girls to:

- Be accepted by the group and regarded with affection by others.

- Gain a sense of control over their activities by helping to plan them.

- Feel secure, free from physical as well as social harm.

- Have new adventures—exciting and varied activities to test the limits of their skills and feel a sense of accomplishment.

- Enjoy recognition and approval—to stand out as individuals for the things they do well.

- Share and enjoy leisure-time activities with a positive adult role model.

Important Characteristics of Outdoor Activities

Here are some tips on providing the most effective outdoor experiences for girls:

- Encourage all the girls to take part in lots of outdoor activities. Significant attitude changes occur in girls who have had several outdoor experiences. Both the quality and quantity of outdoor experiences count! There are a wide variety of settings to explore, from zoos and nature centers, to parks and farms. Those who develop the deepest appreciation for the environment are usually those who have had many opportunities to experience the natural world.

- Do activities outdoors, to have the greatest impact on the girls. Videos, computer games, and indoor simulations may be important for some types of learning, but it is not possible to re-create the learning that comes from doing activities outdoors.

- Use a multisensory approach. Encourage girls to use as many senses as possible in each activity. The smell of food cooking outdoors may be familiar, but have they stopped to smell fresh earth, a wildflower, or the air after a rainstorm?

The Girl Scout recognition requirements provide a wide variety of outdoor skill-building activities for girls. This chart shows many of the progressive activities available for girls from Try-Its for Brownie Girl Scouts, to badges for Junior Girl Scouts, to interest projects for Cadette and Senior Girl Scouts.

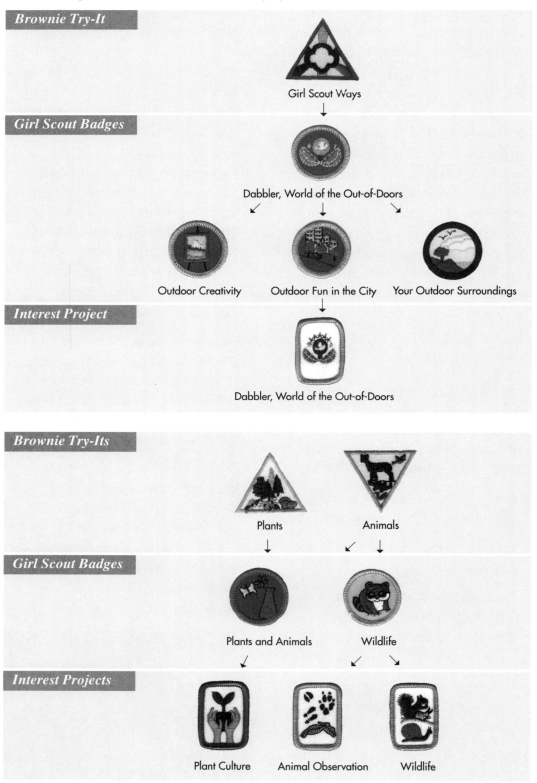

Brownie Try-It

Girl Scout Ways

Girl Scout Badges

Dabbler, World of the Out-of-Doors

Outdoor Creativity   Outdoor Fun in the City   Your Outdoor Surroundings

Interest Project

Dabbler, World of the Out-of-Doors

Brownie Try-Its

Plants   Animals

Girl Scout Badges

Plants and Animals   Wildlife

Interest Projects

Plant Culture   Animal Observation   Wildlife

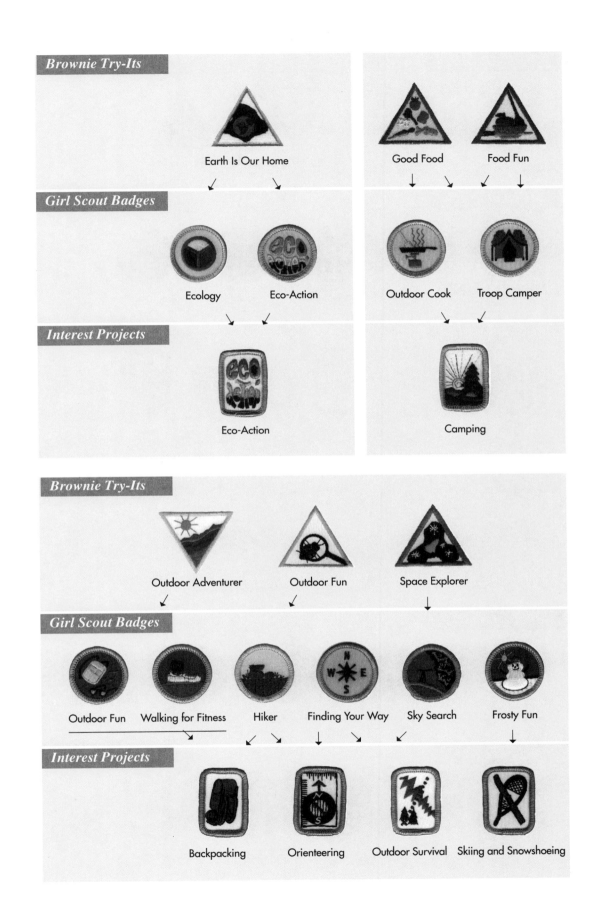

Brownie Try-Its

Earth Is Our Home

Good Food   Food Fun

Girl Scout Badges

Ecology   Eco-Action

Outdoor Cook   Troop Camper

Interest Projects

Eco-Action

Camping

Brownie Try-Its

Outdoor Adventurer   Outdoor Fun   Space Explorer

Girl Scout Badges

Outdoor Fun   Walking for Fitness   Hiker   Finding Your Way   Sky Search   Frosty Fun

Interest Projects

Backpacking   Orienteering   Outdoor Survival   Skiing and Snowshoeing

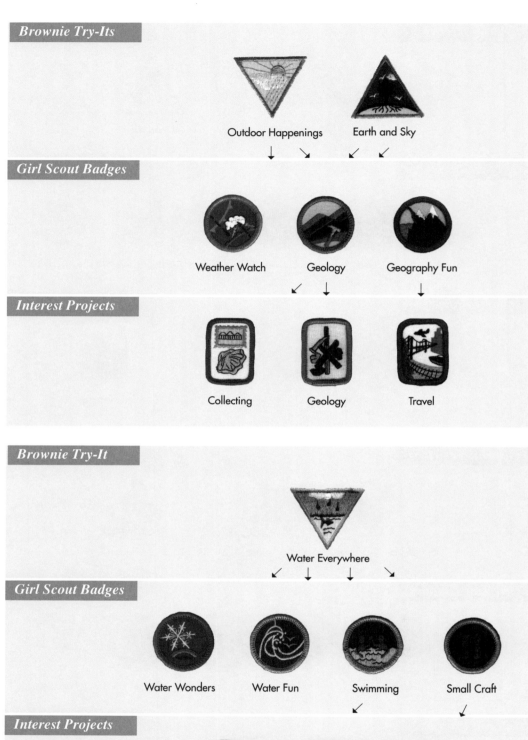

Brownie Try-Its

Outdoor Happenings   Earth and Sky

Girl Scout Badges

Weather Watch   Geology   Geography Fun

Interest Projects

Collecting   Geology   Travel

Brownie Try-It

Water Everywhere

Girl Scout Badges

Water Wonders   Water Fun   Swimming   Small Craft

Interest Projects

Paddle, Pole, and Roll   Water Sports   Smooth Sailing

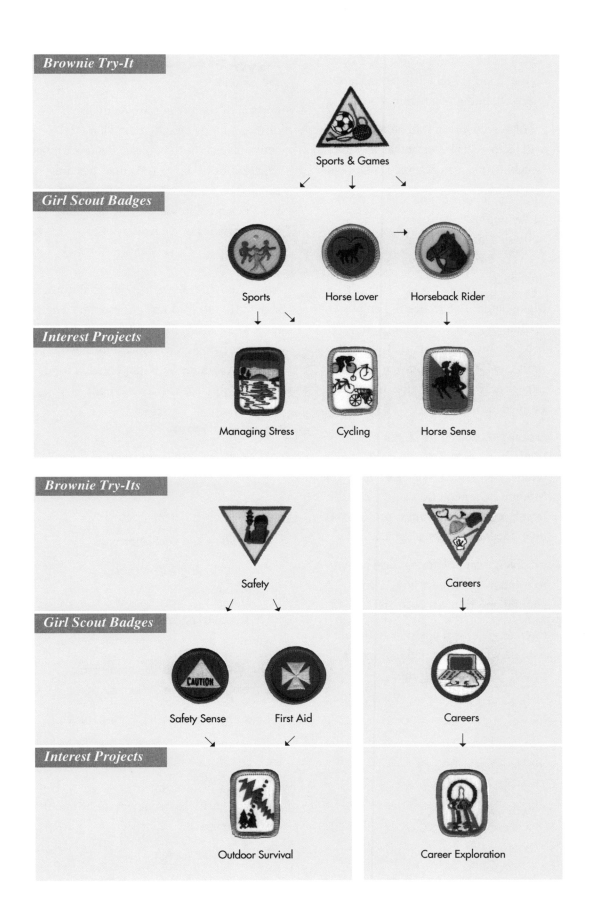

Brownie Try-It

Sports & Games

Girl Scout Badges

Sports   Horse Lover   Horseback Rider

Interest Projects

Managing Stress   Cycling   Horse Sense

Brownie Try-Its

Safety   Careers

Girl Scout Badges

Safety Sense   First Aid   Careers

Interest Projects

Outdoor Survival   Career Exploration

- Teach using authentic objects. Ask girls to touch and smell a leaf, then learn more about the plant from a book.

- Involve each girl in skill building; she will learn skills better in that way than by watching others or reading about them.

- Show the interrelationships of elements in the outdoors. Discuss how outdoor activities affect the land or how some types of birds depend on trees for food and shelter.

- Make outdoor activities fun and challenging, and different from activities done elsewhere. Focus on individual interests and first-hand experiences. The activities then have built-in motivation.

- Do only those activities that have minimal impact on the natural environment. Pack out everything you brought in, whether on a picnic at the beach or a backpacking trip. Remove all evidence of your presence.

- Involve girls in planning each activity to promote positive attitudes and strengthen girl/adult partnerships.

- Provide girls with positive adult role models who can set and maintain a positive tone in the group.

Age-Level Characteristics of Girls

Girls at different ages are ready for different kinds of activities. Plan activities that fit the physical and learning capabilities of the girls so that they are fun and challenging, but not frustrating. Here is a quick review of the general characteristics of each Girl Scout age level.

Note: Activities for girls with disabilities should fit into the same chronological age level as activities for nondisabled girls of the same age. Some adaptations may be necessary, but the activities should closely parallel those for nondisabled girls.

Daisy Girl Scouts

- Have a short attention span.

- Want to do things for themselves.

- Are friendly, helpful, cooperative.

- Need adult and peer approval.

- Are developing fine motor coordination.

- Understand more than can be verbalized.

- Question lots of things about their environment; want to know why.

- Learn by doing, experiencing, playing.

- Are curious.

- Like to collect things.

- Cannot easily see a viewpoint different from their own.

- Like to make things.

Brownie Girl Scouts

- Have better control of large muscles than smaller ones.

- Like to join groups, but often need individual attention.

- Can cut and paste, hammer and tie things.

- Are learning to read and write, developing copying skills.

- Are developing number concepts, beginning time and distance concepts.

- Like to start projects—may not finish them.

- Can remember and do things in a sequence of commands.

- Have limited understanding of abstract words.

- Love to playact.

- Want to assume responsibility.

- Are usually very cooperative.

- Reflect values, attitudes, and prejudices of family.

Junior Girl Scouts

- Have good manual and manipulative skills.

- Have good eye-hand coordination.

- Like peer group activities—friendships are important.

- Are mastering concepts of time and distance.

- Can express abstract ideas in poetry, drawings, songs.

- Begin to show special talents—art, music, etc.

- Take personal pride in completion of their own projects.

- Assume responsibility for their own acts.

- Wish to be helpful.

- Question values and attitudes—start to set their own.
- Can apply logic—can understand some abstract concepts.
- Develop pronounced hero worship.

Cadette Girl Scouts

- Are undergoing rapid physical growth and development.
- Are self-conscious about body image.
- Have increased appetite.
- Need more physical activity.
- Are prone to peer pressure.
- Maintain close, supportive relationships with friends.
- Idolize public figures, e.g., rock stars, teachers, leaders.
- Seek more privacy.
- Test imposed limits.
- Develop own sense of values, influenced by peers.
- Can use logic and alternatives to solve problems.
- Are able to plan ahead.

Senior Girl Scouts

- Have emerging sexual feelings.
- Are interested in clothing and appearance.
- Are able to think abstractly.
- Are able to organize their ideas orally and in writing.
- Develop goals and values.
- Are able to formulate complex plans.
- Often take high risks, thinking themselves immune from consequences.
- Are passionate about beliefs and causes.
- Show anxiety and guilt in conflicts between parents and peers.
- Seek acceptance from peers, but are becoming more independent.
- Have friendships that will last longer.
- Are often over-committed.
- Enjoy family activities but still prefer peers.

The next chapter provides suggestions for taking a group on its first outdoor excursions.

Chapter 2

Stepping into the Outdoors

Rachel Carson, naturalist and author of The Silent Spring, *said that when teaching children about nature, "It is not half so important to know as to feel." Children have an innate and insatiable curiosity about the natural world; they are born scientists! Leaders who guide girls through experiences that allow them to make* their own *discoveries create an atmosphere in which inquiry is stimulating and fun. This approach to learning is called "guided inquiry" and does not require that a leader possess any special knowledge, just enthusiasm and curiosity. The heart of science is not a collection of memorized facts; it is problem-solving, which allows girls to become independent thinkers. You don't have to be an "expert" because* knowing *is not as important as learning* how *to find out.*

Nature Is Everywhere

Settled into our daily routines, we may fail to observe nature's patterns and remarkable details. We may also take for granted the various structures and systems we have created that make modern life possible. There are many things waiting to be discovered right in the sidewalks, trees, schoolyards, and backyards we pass every day. Finding out what they are can be fun and can lead to a deeper understanding of the world in which we live.

Our own neighborhoods are great outdoor classrooms, with laboratories as big as a park or as small as a window box. Neighborhood explorations help children realize that nature is right at their doorstep, no matter where they live, and can be an important first step in helping children feel confident in the outdoors. And studies have shown that children who have repeated exposure to nature, even in an urban setting, develop positive attitudes toward nature and are more likely to become environmentally responsible citizens.

Neighborhood Explorations

Activity Suggestion

Neighborhood Mapping

Creating a map of the neighborhood near the meeting place is a great way for the group to start learning about the natural and human-built components of the environment and how they affect each other. A map can serve as the foundation for the rest of your outdoor science activities, something that can be added to as you explore past the boundaries of your block and expand the frontiers of your curiosity. It could become a valuable

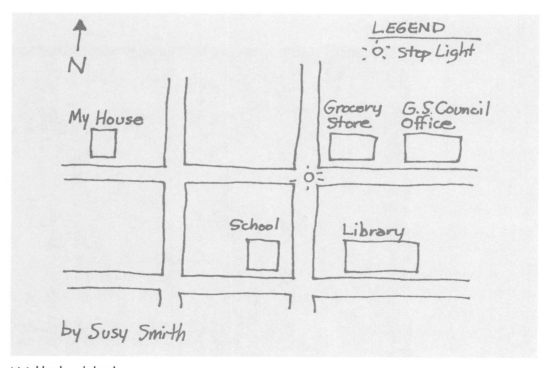

Neighborhood sketch map.

resource for your community if displayed in a public area. Plan a series of short explorations from the troop's meeting place or a convenient place in the area. Help girls to look, listen, feel, and learn by asking questions about the things they see during these activities.

The neighborhood map may include the following components:

1. Human-built environment

Buildings—houses, apartment buildings, banks, supermarkets, shops, schools, libraries, places of worship, community centers, sports centers.

Infrastructures—streets, highways, bridges.

Utilities—fire hydrants, sewers, traffic lights, aerial electrical cables, telephone wires.

2. Natural environment

Plants—weeds, street trees.

Parks, vacant lots, other green spaces.

Water sources—streams, lakes, oceans.

People—their location and activities.

Animals—wild and domestic.

Note the age level, maturity, and degree of curiosity of the girls before planning an activity. If you work with Daisy or Brownie Girl Scouts, you may want to construct your neighborhood map by focusing on a different topic each time you meet. For example, the first activity may be as simple as taking a walk around the neighborhood and jotting down the name of each street you will be using to conduct your investigations. This is a good way of orienting the girls to the location and having them begin to notice things of interest along the way. The directions and major landmarks visible throughout the area can be discussed at this time, too. Next week you may decide to investigate the plant life of the neighborhood or survey the resident animals.

Activity Suggestions

Theme Walks

Go on a theme walk to investigate and collect information about the area.

Alphabet walk. Look for animals, plants, rocks, or other components of the neighborhood that begin with each letter of the alphabet:

A for ants, asphalt, air conditioning units

B for bakery, bricks, birds

C for cats, clover, clouds (etc.)

Color quiz. Find as many colors as possible on your block, or find a color that matches a paint chip or some item each person is wearing.

Shape or architecture hike. Find some of the following shapes in nature or in the built environment: triangles, squares, circles, ovals, rectangles, spirals, and hexagons.

Career survey. See how many careers the girls can associate with the different elements of the area, for example:

- Plants—gardener, landscape architect, farmer.
- Birds—naturalist, wildlife artist, ornithologist.
- Fire hydrant—engineer, firefighter.
- Hospital—doctor, nurse, physical therapist.

Sound hunt. Find a place in a park or open area where troop members can sit for a few minutes with their eyes closed. Listen for all kinds of sounds.

- Morning sounds, evening sounds, day sounds.
- Sounds of the season, sounds nearby or far away.
- Sounds they like, or dislike.
- Occasional and constant sounds.
- Sounds from living things and sounds from machines.

Follow a sound to find out what makes it.

Habitat hunt. Spot as many different animal and plant homes as you can.

Activity Suggestion
Safari

Go on a "safari." Divide your group into Path Finders (responsible for "blazing" the trail everyone else will follow and recording data), Plant Detectives (in charge of finding as many plants as possible), and Animal Investigators (responsible for spotting all the animals in the area). Question for discussion: Should dogs, cats, and humans be included here? Don't forget to look in the cracks and seams of sidewalks, and check crevices and crannies in the bark of trees.

Activity Suggestion
Blueprint of a Block

Ask each girl to make a small-scale drawing of her block that includes natural features, such as grass and trees, and human-built materials and structures, such as buildings and pavement. Next, ask each girl to design the kind of block she would like to live in. Have everyone share her "blueprint" and discuss the choices she has made.

Birds

The sound hunt (above left) may lead you to following the sounds of birds. Sounds are a great way to locate birds and observe their activities.

You can also enjoy watching birds for their colors, behavior, and flight patterns. The great variety of shapes and sizes of bills, legs, feet, and bodies allows birds to thrive in a wide range of habitats. Some birds move in groups and interact with each other constantly. Other types of birds feed, rest, and fly in a solitary manner. Some of these patterns change dramatically during nesting time or migration season. Girls can find a book about birds in the library and learn how to identify the ones common to their area.

Activity Suggestion

Bird Behavior

Have the girls keep journals of their observations of birds common in the area. Do all the girls observe the same behaviors? Can they tell what the birds are communicating to each other with each call or posture?

Activity Suggestion

Bird Feeder Visitors

Hang homemade bird feeders (reuse plastic bottles or juice or milk cartons) outside a window at your meeting place. Observe the birds that come to visit. Are all the birds year-round residents, or have some traveled from faraway lands? Pick a couple of migratory birds and learn the routes they have traveled to delight you

with their presence. Discuss the implications of destroying green spaces along their migration routes.

Other Animals Large and Small

Sometimes it helps to use techniques that slow us down long enough to look very carefully. We find all kinds of things that we usually walk right by.

Activity Suggestion

Focus the View

Bring several wire coat hangers on the next hike. Stretch them into circles and give one to each small group of girls. Have the girls put them on the ground and

carefully examine what they find within the wire circle. Have a few empty plastic pill bottles handy. Girls can put small "finds" into a bottle. Girls can watch the activity of a small bug, see all its parts, and then let it go, or collect seeds, pebbles, or other interesting things they find.

Activity Suggestion

The Animal Viewpoint

Crawl on the ground and look at things from an animal's point of view. Look for evidence of the presence of animals, such as nests, chewed bits of food like acorns and berries, footprints in mud or snow, or holes in leaves, trees, or in the ground.

Activity Suggestion

The Forest Floor

Find the small creatures that live on the forest floor of a wooded area. Are they on logs, leaf litter, or on bare ground? Why? Research the role these animals play in the forest ecosystem. Why are they important?

Trees

Trees and the other green plants around us are vital to life. They make the oxygen that we and other animals consume with every breath as well as providing food, shade, and sources for products we use every day.

Activity Suggestion

Tree Safari Game

Go on a tree safari around your meeting place and play the game shown below. As each activity is completed, cross out that square.

Find a tree that has blossoms on it, and watch them turn into seeds.	Find a nest and two insects in a tree.	Draw a picture of a tree.	Free space	Watch a tree in a windstorm.
Free space	Watch a tree in a rainstorm.	Collect seeds from a tree and plant some.	Find a tree that has changed something else.	Eat a food that comes from a tree.
Find a tree shaped by humans and a tree shaped by nature.	Estimate the height and circumference of a tree taller than you are.	Free space	Do leaf and bark rubbings.	Plant a tree and care for it.
Write a poem about a tree.	Make something useful from a piece of wood.	Watch a tree in a snow- or sand-storm.	Do something to help a tree.	Free space
Name three things that a tree needs in order to grow.	Free space	Examine tree scars to find evidence that the tree has repaired an injury.	Find the oldest and the youngest trees in your neighborhood.	Take a photograph of a tree.

Activity Suggestion

Adopting Trees

Adopt some street trees in your community. Clear away any litter around them and loosen the soil in the tree pits to allow water to reach down to the roots. Get a qualified person to prune any dead branches. Compare how your adopted trees do as opposed to the other ones on your block not receiving any TLC (tender loving care). Do your trees grow bigger, have more flowers, or attract more wildlife?

Activity Suggestion

Animals and Trees— Recording Observations

Keep a log of which animals depend on trees for food, shelter, and raising their young. Does this change with the seasons? Be sure to give the girls time to make observations and drawings and to write down their thoughts every time your troop or group meets.

Soil compaction.

Of Rocks, Minerals, and Water

Soil, water, and air provide the nutrients that plants and animals need to grow. Explore the ways that rocks, soil, and water support life.

Activity Suggestion

Examining Soil

Find a spot to investigate the soil. Provide girls with a small trowel and let them dig a hole in the soil. Look for color changes and layers. Measure the depth of different layers. Feel the soil. Rub some moist soil between thumb and fingers. If it feels gritty, then it is composed mainly of relatively large particles of sand and is called sandy soil. If it feels smooth and very sticky, it is clay soil. If it feels smooth and not sticky, it is called loam soil. See Chapter 7 for more information on soil.

Activity Suggestion

Soil Compaction

Push a pencil into the soil with the open palm of your hand. Measure the distance it has gone into the soil when the hand begins to hurt. Try this in different areas, including places where people walk or play frequently. How do the measurements vary?

Percolation Test: How the Soil Absorbs Water

Push a soup-size can (without ends) into the soil about one inch. Fill the can with water and count the number of seconds (or minutes) it takes for the soil to absorb the water. Try this in different areas.

This activity and the previous one show that there is air space in soil. The water fills up the air space until it drains through the soil. Sandy soil has bigger air spaces than clay soil. When soil is walked on quite often it becomes compacted, losing the air space, and water cannot sink in. Then puddles form or the water flows away if it lands on a slope.

After doing this activity, ask girls to explain why puddles form under playground equipment or in certain places in paths, backyards, and parks.

Soil percolation.

Activity Suggestion

Identifying Building Materials

Sidewalks and buildings may be made of natural materials (for example, slate, granite, limestone, clay). Can you spot any of these in your town? Find out where these materials come from and how they were formed. Let the girls plan an expedition, including the route. (You may want to set boundaries, depending on the age of the girls and safety concerns.)

Activity Suggestion

Drinking Water Sources

Do you know where your drinking water comes from? Highlight the importance of watersheds (all the land drained by a river) by tracing the path of a drop of water as it travels from its source on uplands or a mountain, to the faucet in your home. Many things happening in the area of the watershed can affect the quality of the water. Can your troop think of ways in which each girl can conserve water at home, or improve the quality of our drinking water?

Activity Suggestion

Waste Water Treatment

What happens to the water used in our homes? Take a trip to a sewage treatment plant to find out what happens to water after it goes down the drain. What things should not be put into drains?

Become a Question-Asker

As girls continue to explore their environment, the leader can help by asking appropriate questions. By becoming a "question-asker" instead of a "question-answerer," leaders can teach girls *how* to think, not *what* to think. Leaders also will be using a good technique for problem-solving that lets them become partners in their girls' discoveries. This new role will allow the leader to support, guide, and monitor the group, while allowing each girl to be responsible for her own learning. Learning by self-discovery allows room for personal expression and individual learning styles. The message that "your way is OK" will make science fun and build self-confidence not only in the girls, but in leaders, too!

Some questions can be used to determine the progress of a girl or her level of ability. Other questions help create a thinking atmosphere and help the girls get used to supporting their statements with

reasons. Basically, there are two types of questions: closed-ended and open-ended.

Closed-Ended Questions

These questions involve thinking skills such as knowledge and comprehension and generally invoke replies that are short, can be answered by "yes" or "no," or have one "right" answer.

Knowledge questions. These questions test for recall of information, such as dates, terms, definitions, or methods and procedures. At this level, girls can be asked to list, identify, name, match, outline, describe, define, or label.

Examples: How many body parts does an insect have? What does the term "metamorphosis" mean?

Comprehension questions. These types of questions can be used to make sure that girls have understood information and not just memorized it. Responses require girls to rephrase information in their own words. Comprehension questions can include the words explain, describe, distinguish, compare, paraphrase, summarize, demonstrate, classify, or illustrate.

Examples: How would you describe a centipede to someone who has never seen one? What are the similarities between spiders and ants? Compare the plant structures of a water lily and an oak tree.

Thinking skills at the knowledge and comprehension levels do not require a great deal of mental effort, but they are important. They lay the foundation for the development of critical thinking skills, such as analysis and evaluation.

For girls who have disabilities that make comprehension difficult, make sure to shorten the questions and simplify language.

Open-Ended Questions

Open-ended questions require responses that are thoughtful, analytical, and evaluative. Because they elicit expressions of individual perceptions and ideas, open-ended questions help build confidence and self-esteem. This encourages dialogue not only between the leader and the girls but, more importantly, between girls.

Analysis questions. These questions can be used to distinguish between facts and opinions, show how something is put together by looking at individual components, show the underlying structure of something, or identify implications and motives.

Examples: What might have been the motives of author Rachel Carson in writing *The Silent Spring*? What do you think would happen if the government imposed tougher recycling regulations? Given a description of an experiment conducted by a team, describe how the steps of the scientific method worked to produce a valid experiment.

Evaluation questions. These questions require making decisions on controversial topics and backing them up with sound reasons, and making judgments on the validity of sources.

Examples: If you were going to repeat a water quality experiment, how would you do it better? Should an endangered species be saved from extinction at the expense of local jobs? What do you think of people who hunt for sport?

The Art of Questioning

Mastering the art of asking questions takes time and practice. Prepare ahead of time by planning a series of questions for each activity, but be flexible enough to revise questions as the need arises. It is best to use a mix of question types. Starting an activity with closed-ended questions can help girls review prior information and focus on the specifics of their pending investigation. Gradually build up to open-ended questions that elicit a broad spectrum of information and involve the girls in thinking creatively and critically.

It is important to give some positive feedback to each girl who answers, regardless of whether the answer is correct. A child who is told that her answer is wrong may feel discouraged from making further contributions. Replying with "You're partly right, but consider…" will reward a girl for her attempt to think things through, while guiding her in the right direction.

Studies have shown that teachers who dominate classroom verbal interactions

create an environment in which students become passive learners and exhibit less imagination, creativity, and thinking skills. By comparison, students who are encouraged to ask questions become more involved in their learning and use high-level thinking skills.

Conducting an Investigation

Unanswered questions can lead girls to design an investigation to find their own answers. Here are five steps to take in conducting an investigation.

Step 1: Choose the question or topic to investigate. Example: How do birds communicate?

Step 2: Predict the results. Ask girls to predict what they will find out. Example: Different kinds of birds will communicate in different ways.

Step 3: Plan the investigation or experiment. Explain how you will collect the information you think you will need in order to answer the question or solve the problem. Example: Birdseed will be scattered in the same place every day for two weeks to attract birds common in the neighborhood. While the birds feed, observations of their displays (sounds and gestures) will be recorded at the same time for ten minutes every other day for one month.

Step 4: Collect and record the data. Determine how the data will be recorded. Example: Observations will be recorded on a two-column chart, one for drawings or descriptions of each observed behavior and the other for what the behavior appears to communicate.

Step 5: Draw conclusions. Review your observations. Example: Could you tell what was being communicated by each display you observed? Some related

questions might be: Did all species of birds use the same displays to communicate the same message? Did both males and females of the same species exhibit the same displays?

Compare your prediction in Step 2 with the results. What did you learn?

Activity Suggestion

Impact of Park Visitors

What plants and animals live in or depend on a pond or lake in a local park or botanical garden? Does anything that park visitors do affect the quality of life of these creatures? If so, what can your troop do to educate people about this? What other topics will the girls wish to investigate? Use the steps on the previous page to investigate one of these questions.

Helping girls discover that the natural and human-built worlds are inextricably intertwined can make a big difference in how each one perceives her surroundings and, more importantly, herself. A positive sense of self and place can empower girls to improve the quality of their lives. Girls who actively participate in community projects will be better prepared to solve environmental problems.

Field Trip Tips

1. Use your girls' experiences and interests as a guide for choosing a topic to investigate. Although the topic will provide the framework for the investigation, be flexible enough to take advantage of "teachable moments."

2. Become familiar with the area you have chosen to use. Make sure the site is safe and appropriate for the type of activity you wish to conduct. Learn to recognize and avoid poisonous plants—such as poison ivy, oak, or sumac—and determine whether protection from insects or other animals is needed.

3. Establish physical boundaries for the study area. This will give young girls the safety boundaries necessary for them to be actively involved in the experience.

4. Familiarize the girls ahead of time with any procedures and equipment you will be using. For example, if you will be studying the health of a local pond, make sure the girls know how to use any water quality test kits (appropriate for their age level) that the activity calls for. And be sure to review safety precautions for activities near the water.

5. Have fun!

Activity Suggestion

Bird Census

Question/topic: How many different birds can you find in the block around your meeting place?

Prediction: Ask the girls to predict, based on their experience, how many kinds of birds they think they will find.

Plan: Pair the girls and ask each team to spot as many birds as it can. Asking the following guiding questions will help the girls focus on the activity and stimulate their thinking: Are there more of one kind of bird than another? How can you tell? Where did you find each bird? What do you think it was doing there?

Collection and recording of data: Each team should make a chart using a sheet of paper folded into three columns—the first for a drawing or description of each type of bird, the second for noting the place(s) each kind of bird was found, and the last for recording the number of each type of bird seen. Give the girls time indoors to put the finishing touches on their charts.

Conclusions: Have each team share the results and conclusions.

Suggested materials/equipment:

- Paper for chart.

- Pencils, crayons, or colored markers.

- Clipboards (a piece of cardboard and a paper clip will do nicely).

- Books on birds.

Local resources you can tap:

- Audubon Society chapter.

- Zoo.

- College/university biology department.

- Department of Parks and Recreation.

- Natural history museum.

- Conservation groups active in your area.

Chapter 3

Learning Outdoor Skills

Learning skills that will be helpful in the outdoors can start during any troop meeting and, along with a progressive series of trips, can provide the group with the skills to travel almost anywhere. Girls can start with short, local experiences and then dream about trips to come! Many of these skills are also useful when a natural disaster hits near home. Knowing how to do without the conveniences of modern life is a survival skill.

3

Dressing for the Weather

Faced with varying weather conditions in the outdoors, girls must be able to select and care for outdoor clothing and be prepared for sudden changes in temperature. Dressing appropriately can ensure well-being in cold or hot weather.

It is important to be familiar with layering, the basic principle of dressing for the outdoors. Layering involves wearing layers of garments rather than one or two heavy ones. Each layer must provide warmth and ventilation without hindering mobility. Layering helps the body regulate temperature in warm or cold weather and can help prevent hypothermia (lowered body temperature) or heat exhaustion.

In cold weather, the first layer should be made of breathable material so that body moisture will not be trapped. The second layer provides insulation and may consist of several pieces of clothing. The final layer should be a jacket that gives protection from wind or moisture.

Knowing the characteristics of different types of fabrics such as wool, cotton, nylon, silk, and synthetic materials will make clothing selection easier. For example, wool provides warmth even when wet while cotton is very good for allowing air circulation, a plus for staying cool.

Here are some general points to consider when selecting appropriate clothing for an activity:

- Wear clothing that allows for freedom of movement during strenuous activity.

- In the cold, a hat helps to retain as much as 40 percent of body heat, and in very sunny weather it protects against the rays of the sun.

Light colors are best in the heat because they reflect the sun's rays. Dark colors are effective in the cold because they absorb heat.

- Dangling or flapping clothing can be a hazard, especially around campfires and stoves. Do not wear flammable clothing such as a plastic raincoat near stoves and fires.

- If there is a chance of getting wet, a water-repellent jacket and pants should be worn, especially on cooler days or when wind will evaporate moisture from the skin. Under these conditions, becoming hypothermic is a real concern.

- Clothing that covers the arms and legs will provide protection from biting insects, ticks, poisonous plants, and sunburn. It also helps guard against bruises and scrapes.

- Properly fitting, sturdy shoes with non-slip soles will protect feet on rugged, rocky terrain.

- To understand why it is important to wear wool clothing rather than cotton in cold weather, try this experiment with the girls:

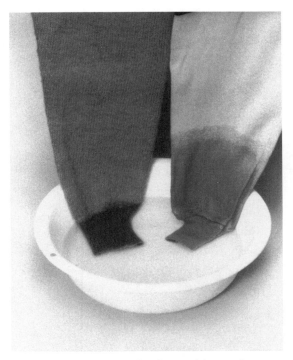

Water does not wick up the sleeve of the wool sweater on the left. Water does travel up a cotton garment, as shown by the sweatshirt on the right. Wool garments help us to stay warm in the winter.

Activity Suggestion

Cotton vs. Wool

Put an old cotton sweatshirt sleeve on one arm and a wool sweater sleeve on the other. (Gloves or socks may also be used.) Place both arms into a pail of water so that the lower parts of the sleeves get wet. Remove arms from the water and decide which arm feels warmer. Watch to see if the wetness creeps up each sleeve. Cotton soaks up water very quickly and remains wet. Wool helps to retain body warmth even when wet. It dries more quickly and sheds water. Therefore, it is more beneficial to wear wool in cold weather.

Activity Suggestion

Foot Warmth

To demonstrate the importance of warm footwear, obtain several large jars of equal size and shape (e.g., pickle or peanut butter jars) and fill each with very hot tap water. Insert each jar into a different kind of sock (nylon stocking, cotton sock, wool sock, etc.). Set the jars outdoors with a thermometer in each. Record water temperature in the jars every five minutes. Which jar cools more quickly? What kind of sock would keep feet warmer?

Activity Suggestion

Outdoor Fashions

Girls can have fun learning about appropriate clothing by dressing up in items they choose from a pile of clothes for particular circumstances. Make a skit, fashion show, or relay race out of it after girls learn the basics.

Finding the Way

Girls can take the basic skills of finding their way around in familiar settings to new environments. When in new places it is important to be able to tell directions, follow a map to explore, and stay oriented to find the way back. Girls can follow a simple map or make a simple sketch map of the neighborhood or of the route to a favorite place. They can also learn how to determine directions for north, south, east, and west from natural signs (see page 102).

Girls may be interested in learning about and using trail signs while exploring the outdoors. Trail signs are used to mark paths for others to follow. While on a hike, girls may want to leave a message so another group can find them. Sticks, stones, twigs, or anything handy may be used. In an emergency, cloth strips could

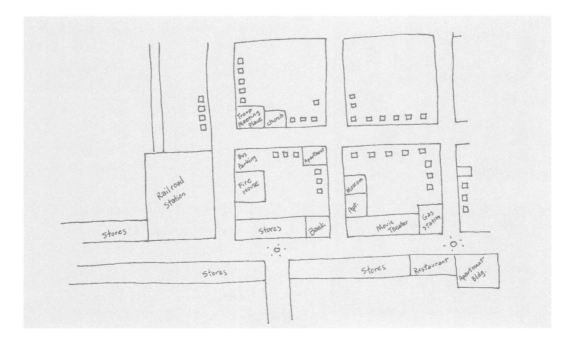

be used. If a trail is not going to be used again, remove any signs the group has created. Some useful trail signs are shown below.

Patrols can practice their skills by laying trails for each other or by trading maps and following them. Chapter 6 provides more information and activities for using maps and compasses.

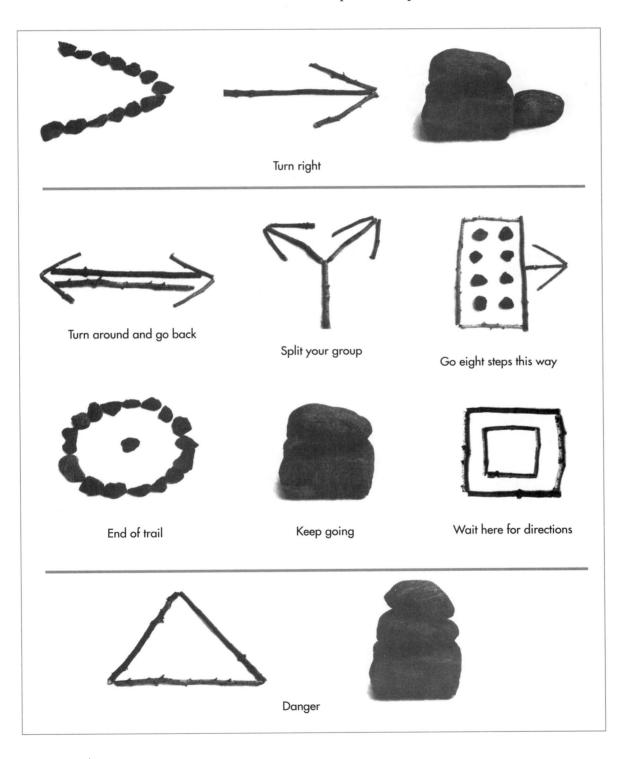

Turn right

Turn around and go back

Split your group

Go eight steps this way

End of trail

Keep going

Wait here for directions

Danger

Water Purification

While planning an outdoor activity, check on the available water supply at the site. Even for a day hike each girl should carry an adequate supply of water. Only water from a tap that has been tested and approved by the local health department can be considered safe to use. Other sources of water such as lakes, streams, or ponds must be purified. Even a sparkling clear river in the wilderness can be contaminated by bacteria, viruses, protozoa, chemicals, dead animals, or unsanitary conditions upstream out of view.

One of the most common and potentially serious gastrointestinal conditions is caused by *Giardia lamblia*, a protozoan found in many rivers and lakes. *Giardia* spreads as a result of the fecal contamination of the water supply by humans and other mammals. Another protozoan is *Cryptosporidium*, which is becoming more prevalent. Both can cause diarrhea, nausea, loss of appetite, cramps, weakness, and vomiting. Victims should receive medical attention as soon as possible since dehydration can be a serious complication.

Since there is no way to know if the drinking water is contaminated, one of the following options must be used to treat water used for drinking, food preparation, brushing teeth, or rinsing dishes. First, if the water is not clear and clean-looking, pour it into another container through a clean cloth or bandanna to filter out solid particles and organic matter. Then use one of the following methods.

Boiling

Boiling water for at least one minute should kill any microorganisms present and make it safe to drink. The water will taste better after boiling if air is added to it. This can be done by pouring it between two clean containers several times to aerate it.

Filtration

Water filtration devices remove tiny particles and microorganisms from the water. Some filters also remove chemicals and bacteria. Viruses are so tiny that no field filtration device can remove them. Filtered water must receive additional chemical treatment to destroy any viruses.

In order to remove *Giardia*, it is critical to purchase a water filter designed to filter out this organism. The maximum pore size of the filter must be 4 microns or less, or else *Giardia* will slip through and contaminate the water. Check the packaging of the filter before buying it to make sure it is designed to filter out *Giardia*.

A hand-pump style filter makes the job quicker and more efficient. Remove water from the source into a container labeled "dirty" and pump it into another container marked "clean." Be sure not to mix up the two containers. Filtered water is ready to drink immediately after filtering. Follow the manufacturer's instructions carefully for filtering, cleaning, and replacing the filter.

Chemical Treatment

Iodine is available in tablet, crystal, or a concentrated form for use in purifying water. The effectiveness of iodine varies with several factors, including the temperature and pH of the water, the amount of time between adding iodine and drinking the water, the clarity of the water, and the shelf life of the product.

Individuals with thyroid conditions and pregnant women should consult their physicians before ingesting iodine. It is available in camping supply stores and drugstores. Follow the manufacturer's instructions carefully.

Water should not be purified using chlorine. Chlorine reacts with organic materials in the water, hindering the disinfecting process. Household bleach is not recommended since this product was not manufactured to disinfect water. Chlorine tablets are no longer available.

Water filters remove harmful microorganisms from water.

Eating Right

Younger girls or inexperienced campers may learn basic cooking skills at home or at a series of cookouts in a backyard or park. The next step may be using an electric or gas stove while cabin camping. While tent camping, girls may cook on a two- or three-burner cookstove. Food preparation on a stove is easy, quick, and allows more time for other program activities.

Good nutrition and drinking plenty of fluids are essential to any outdoor activity. When anyone is working hard and becomes very tired, it is easy to forget to replenish fluids or eat properly. A well-nourished person is more likely to be healthy, energetic, aware, and strong. A day hike, overnight, or extended trip will be enhanced if food selection and preparation are done thoughtfully and carefully. Sufficient food for each person is critical. Everyone going on the trip should take an active role in planning the menu. Considerations include:

- The level of physical activity planned and the sizes of appetites (it helps to determine the number of calories needed per day).

- The kind of weather expected. More calories are needed in very cold weather if outdoor activities are planned.

- Sources of food—from products purchased at a grocery store to specially made freeze-dried products for outdoor cooking.

- Food preferences—likes and dislikes. Check with persons in the group to determine food allergies and religious or other restrictions for some foods. Provide enough selection of foods to accommodate everyone.

- Method and space for transporting food. The selections may be very different if the food is being carried from a car to a cabin rather than taken on the hike.

- Amount of space available for refrigeration.

- Nutritionally balanced menus.

- Amount of money to be spent on food.

- Facility for food preparation.

- Time to experiment with some different foods and food preparations.

The energy supplied by food is measured in calories, which are units of heat. A day hike on flat land has a different caloric demand than climbing a steep mountain while carrying a heavy backpack. In cold weather, a person requires more calories. Calories are best obtained by eating a balanced variety of foods containing carbohydrates, fats, and proteins. Most of the high-energy foods needed for hard, physical work can be found in the starches and sugars of carbohydrates. So, don't forget to pack high-energy snacks such as dried fruit, nuts, cheese, and chocolate.

Drinking fluids is very important. A dehydrated person may have headaches, nausea, or muscle cramps. If a person becomes dehydrated, depending upon the conditions, the chances of getting heatstroke, altitude illness, or hypothermia are increased. In order to stay well hydrated, each person should drink water with every meal. Water should be consumed frequently throughout the day, even when the individual is not thirsty. Some drinks such as colas, tea, and coffee act as diuretics, so they are not good substitutes for water. Monitor fluid intake and elimination. Urine should be clear or pale yellow. If the urine is dark yellow, drink more fluids.

Shopping for Food

Shopping for the trip is an important experience for the girls. Encourage girls to comparison shop. Read labels, determine the nutritional value, weight, cooking time, and cost of items. Terms such as "instant," "quick-cooking," "pre-cooked," "partially pre-cooked," or "just add water" indicate that the food item may be prepared quickly. Food selection can be more varied if weight and cooking time are not important factors. If the girls are camping at an established site, greater varieties of foods can be chosen, including fresh foods and refrigerated items.

Packaging Food

The food purchased for a trip can be repackaged into meal- or patrol-sized servings and packed by the meal and day. Reduce the weight by leaving excess packaging at home and repacking some foods into plastic bags that seal across the top. Be sure to include the directions for cooking.

Protecting Food from Animals

When staying inside a building or cabin, store food in a refrigerator or in containers and rodent-proof cabinets so that mice or other small animals cannot chew through packaging. Mice will even nibble on a bar of soap. At an established campsite, store food inside rodent-proof areas, if available, or in a vehicle. Girls must be cautioned not to keep any food in their tents, duffel bags, or packs. Mice and other animals will chew through clothing and packs to get to the food. Careful cleanup will help to keep away unwanted ants and other insects.

Dishwashing at an Established Site

Dishwashing for a group in an established setting works most efficiently with a little planning. Water can be conserved by using the following hints. To make pots used for cooking over a fire easier to clean, rub soap over the bottom and sides of the *outside* of the pots *before* placing them on the fire. A bar of soap or liquid dishwashing soap can be used. Scrape plates and presoak pots before washing. Heat dishwater on the camp stove or cooking fire so it will be ready when the meal is finished. Keep the dishwater clean as long as possible by washing the least dirty items such as cups and silverware first, and pots last.

Use three buckets or deep pans for dishwashing. The first bucket contains hot, soapy water; the second bucket contains clean water for rinsing; and the third contains boiling water, or cool water containing a sanitizing solution approved by the local health department. Sanitize dishes by immersing them in clear boiling water for one minute or by immersing them in a sanitizing solution in accordance with the directions.

Use individual net bags to hold dishes during the final sterilizing rinse. Hang up the net bags to air dry. If a clothesline is put up for the net bags, be sure that it is away from dust and areas where someone might walk into it and be injured. When dry, dishes and eating utensils should be stored away from dust.

Used dishwater should be filtered to remove any food particles. Place the filtered food particles in the garbage. At an established site, use a sink or waste-water dumping area for disposal of the dishwater.

Net bags are used to air dry dishes and eating utensils.

Knots

Knots can be used for a variety of camp needs such as tying up a sleeping bag or putting up a clothesline. More advanced campers will use knots for setting up tents or securing a boat to a dock, for example. Knowing how to tie knots, what each knot is used for, and the strength of each knot is important. There are more than 8,000 different knots to tie! Six common knots are illustrated on pages 43–45.

To prevent nylon or plastic rope from fraying, the ends should be burned so the fibers melt together. This should be done under adult supervision. Blow out the flame when the end is fused.

Another alternative is whipping. It is usually used on rope made of natural fibers.

Whipping a Rope

1. To whip a rope, a piece of string 8 to 12 inches is needed. Make a loop at one end of the string and lay the loop along the rope with the ends of the string hanging off the end of the rope. Use fingers to hold this loop of string in place.

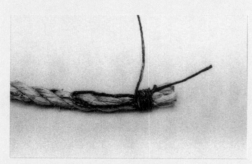

2. Wind the long end of the string tightly over the loop and around the rope. The short end of the string will be left hanging.

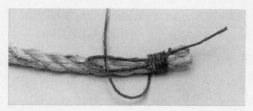

3. Wind the string around the rope for about one inch. Generally, the length of the whipping should be about the same as the diameter of the rope. Wind tightly but do not overlap the strands of the string. Tuck the end of the string that has been wound through the loop. Hold it with the thumb so it will not loosen.

4. Pull slowly on the other end of the string.

5. The loop will disappear under the winding. Pull until the loop is halfway under the winding. Trim off the ends to make a neat whipping.

Half Hitch

The half hitch is a simple turn used to fasten the end of a rope after it has been looped around something such as a post or through a ring.

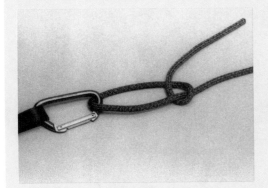

Loop the end of the rope around the post or through the ring. Make a half hitch by looping the short end of the rope under the long end and through the space created.

Make a second half hitch beyond the first half hitch, and you have two half hitches. Two half hitches make a sliding knot that moves along the standing part of the rope. The sliding knot is used to change the tension on the rope without retying the knot each time.

Overhand Knot

The overhand knot is useful for tying shoes, or at the end of another knot to keep it from working free.

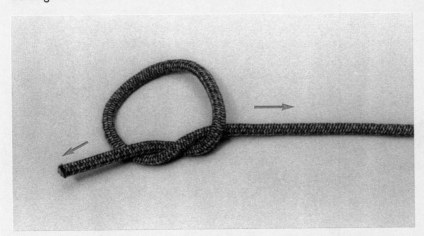

1. Make a loop and bring one end around the rope and through the loop.

2. Pull the ends of the rope tightly.

Clove Hitch

The clove hitch is used to fasten one end of a rope around a post or tree. For instance, the clove hitch could be used when putting up a clothesline between two trees. If kept taut, the knot will not slip.

Pass the short end of the rope around the back of the post or tree. Bring the short end around in front and cross it over the long part of the rope, making an "X."

Hold the "X" with your thumb and forefinger while you wrap the rope around the post again below the first turn. Push the rope end under the "X," so that the end comes out between the two turns around the post. Pull the short end with one hand and the long end with the other. As long as there is a steady pull on the long end, the hitch will not loosen.

Taut-line Hitch

The taut-line hitch is used to make a loop that is adjustable in length. The hitch slides along the standing part of the rope and is useful in adjusting the tension on a tent rope.

Loop the short end of the rope around the tent peg. Wind the short end of the rope around the standing part twice.

Fasten the short end to the standing part with a half hitch above the previous loops. The tension on the rope can be easily adjusted by sliding the knot along the rope.

Bowline

The bowline is used at the end of a rope to form a loop that will remain the same size. The knot can be used to form a loop over a peg or hook or to make a loop around a post, a tree, or a person's waist.

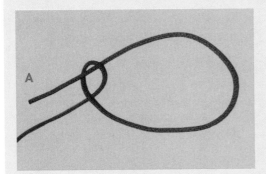

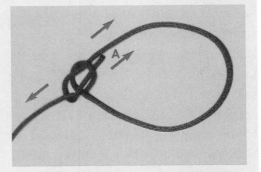

Make a small loop by passing the working end over the standing end of the rope. (The length of the rope from this loop to the end of the working portion of the rope will be the approximate circumference of the final loop that will be formed.) Bring end A up through the loop.

Pass end A beneath the standing part of the rope. Push end A down through the loop again. Tighten up pulling on the standing and working ends of the rope.

Square Knot

The square knot is used to join two ropes of the same thickness. It is also used to tie a bandage in place. To make a square knot, use two pieces of rope.

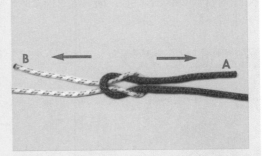

Hold one end of each rope in each hand. Cross end A over end B, then push it under and up behind.

Then cross A over B again, pushing A around and under B and up through the loop. Tighten by pulling both loose ends.

Jackknives

A jackknife is a knife with at least one folding blade that can be used for a wide variety of tasks, including cutting a rope, scraping a carrot, or creating tinder to start a fire. Some jackknives have more than one blade and an assortment of tools such as an awl for drilling holes, a can opener, or a combination screwdriver and bottle-cap opener. For safety, only one blade or tool should be opened at a time. A jackknife must be handled responsibly and used properly to ensure the safety of the users, other people in the immediate area, and the environment. Everyone needs to learn how to use a knife safely and how to take care of, maintain, and store it in good condition. Even girls who are blind or visually impaired can learn to use a knife. It is especially important that girls handle knives that are sharp, since a dull knife will cut more erratically, will be harder to control, and therefore has the potential to cause greater injury.

Some tips for using the jackknife are:

- Move at least an arm's length away from anyone else before using a jackknife.

- Hold the handle securely with the whole hand.

- Always cut away from the body.

- Keep the jackknife closed when not in use.

- Do not walk around with an open jackknife.

- Keep the jackknife away from extreme cold or heat; either will ruin the metal and plastic components of the knife.

- Use the jackknife responsibly. Find more positive ways to remember a trip than vandalizing a site by carving on a picnic table or on live trees.

Opening a Jackknife

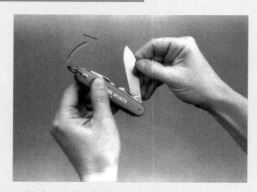

Hold the jackknife firmly with the fingers of one hand. Hold the top edge (slot) of the blade with your thumb and forefinger. Keep your fingers away from the sharp cutting edge of the blade. Pull the blade all the way out until it clicks into its open position.

Closing a Jackknife

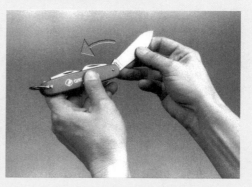

Hold the handle in one hand with the sharp cutting side of the blade upward. Hold the dull, noncutting side of the blade in the other hand. Push the blade up and around toward the slot in the handle.

Passing the Knife

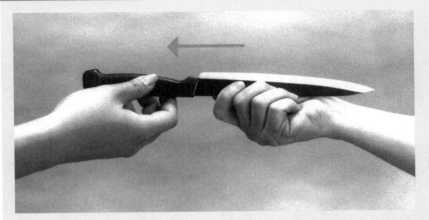

Always close a jackknife before you pass it. When handling other knives, grasp the knife blade along the dull edge and pass the handle to the other person. This way, you have control of the sharp edge of the knife. When not in use, a jackknife must be kept closed and in a pocket or pack.

Sharpening the Knife

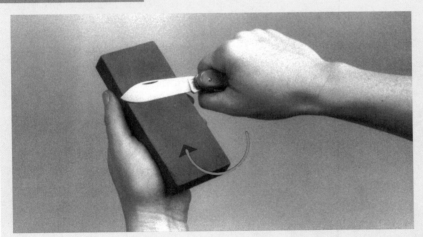

As noted earlier, a sharp knife is safer than a dull knife. Be sure to include a sharpening stone on your list of items to bring. The sharpening stone should be lubricated with oil or water before using. First use the stone's coarse grit to remove nicks, and then use the fine grit to hone the edge to perfection.

1. Hold the stone in one hand and the open jackknife in the other. Keep the fingers holding the stone below the top edge of the sharpening stone.

2. Lay the flat side of the jackknife blade on the flat surface of the stone. The jackknife will be at a slight (15–20 degree) angle to the stone, with the unsharpened edge of the blade slightly raised.

3. Keeping this angle, move the blade across the stone in a circular motion. Make sure the whole edge of the blade is in contact with the stone at some time during the motion.

4. Turn the jackknife over and start again at the base of the blade, repeating the same motion, but in the opposite direction. The jackknife blade and the sharpening stone may become warm from the friction.

5. Test the sharpness of the knife by cutting a piece of rope.

Cleaning the Jackknife

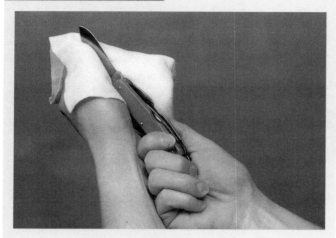

Always keep the jackknife clean and dry.

Hold the cleaning cloth at the back of the blade away from the cutting edge. Wipe the blade clean and dry as you draw the cloth toward the blade's tip. Wipe carefully across the whole blade.

Oiling the Jackknife

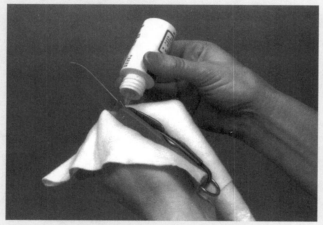

Lubricate the jackknife's hinge with lightweight oil; sewing machine oil is a good choice.

Never clean the blade by rubbing it in dirt or sand.

Cooking Outdoors

In the past, wood fires were often the primary source of heat for cooking for campers. For many reasons this practice is no longer recommended. Heavily used camping areas have become severely damaged as a result of intensive wood gathering; the burned wood is no longer available to rot and add to the richness of the soil. Construction of numerous fire circles and fires built too close to rocks and trees have covered many sites with soot. Disposal of partially burned wood and ash have changed the soil and growing conditions for plants. The smoke reduces air quality and can severely hurt children with asthma and other breathing difficulties. Today, Girl Scouts are strongly encouraged to use alternatives to wood for cooking. Many types of portable camping stoves are available.

Another cooking alternative suitable for troop camping in an established Girl Scout site or recreation area is a solar cooker (see pages 55–56).

Stove Selection

The size and type of stove selected depend upon the location of the activity, the readiness of the girls to use the stove, the number of people being fed, the number and sizes of pots available, and the type of fuel.

A propane stove with two burners is good for group cooking.

Be sure that the stove you select:

- Is designed for use at an established site or is easily transported as needed for the particular activity and age group.

- Is easy and safe to use for the age level of girls using it.

- Uses a type of fuel that can be readily obtained or will be available at the site.

- Will start without elaborate priming procedures.

- Has a suitable cooking capacity, including the size of pots it will hold.

- Has a base wider than the pot support surface so it will not tip over easily.

- Is designed for easy assembly with welded surfaces and a minimum of moving or connecting parts.

- Is designed for easy cleaning.

- Is free from sharp or protruding edges.

- Provides air space between the flame and pot when the flame is high.

- Is strong enough to take long-term use.

- Is built to keep the fuel tank from overheating when the stove is lit.

- Does not tend to flare.

- Will function in below-freezing temperatures or above 6,000 feet if needed.

Determine the number of stoves that will be needed for the size of the group. Be sure to *carefully* save and follow the manufacturer's operating instructions that come with each stove.

Fuel Selection

Choose a stove that uses one of the following fuels.

Propane. Some of the safest and most efficient stoves burn propane, which comes in pressurized tanks. Refueling is easy, a matter of replacing the tank. Propane is dependable at high altitudes and in freezing temperatures. But propane tanks are thicker-walled than butane tanks and too heavy to backpack. Propane is best used during a backyard cookout, at a Girl Scout program site, or in a setting where the tank does not have to be carried more than a short distance.

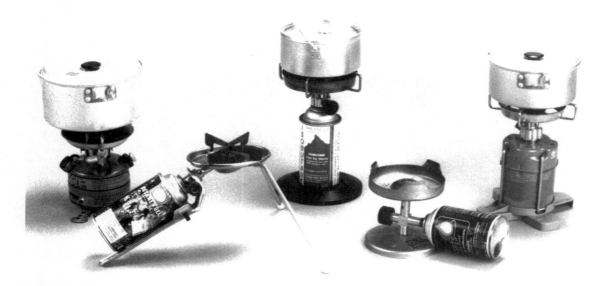

A variety of fuels are used in portable camping stoves.

Butane. This fuel also comes in pressurized tanks. The stove is refueled by replacing the tank. A butane stove burns cleanly and operates easily. Excellent at above-freezing temperatures, butane does not function well in temperatures below freezing and loses some of its efficiency when the fuel supply in the tank gets low. Butane fuel cartridges should be recycled; generally they cannot be refilled.

Blended fuel. A blended fuel of propane and butane is another increasingly popular option that may improve cooking capability in below-freezing conditions.

Gasoline. Most stoves use refined gasoline made specifically for portable stoves. Some stoves burn unleaded gasoline. Gasoline performs best of all these fuels in cold weather and heats water to boiling in the shortest time. Some gasoline stoves must be primed. (Priming is a technique used to pre-warm the burner

to help light the fuel.) The manufacturer of each stove provides specific instructions on how to do this. A highly volatile fuel, gasoline must be used with great care. (Similar products may be known by brand names such as Coleman Fuel.)

Kerosene. A kerosene stove can be set directly on snow or on a cold surface and still operate efficiently. The heat output is high. Kerosene costs only a few pennies per hour to burn; however, it smokes and smells. It does not evaporate quickly and leaves a residue wherever spilled. Kerosene stoves can be difficult to start.

Alcohol. Alcohol burns at low temperatures, producing only half as much heat as kerosene. An alcohol stove is lightweight. Alcohol has low volatility and does not tend to flare, but it can be high-priced and not as easy to locate as other fuels. Since it is not a petroleum product, an alcohol fire can be put out with water.

Sterno. Sterno is safer than liquid fuels and relatively inexpensive, but has low heating power. More Sterno is required to cook a meal than is the case with other types of fuel. Sterno comes in a lightweight, metal container with a replaceable lid.

Stove Efficiency

The following factors influence stove efficiency:

- *Altitude.* The higher the altitude, the longer the cooking time. It takes twice as long to boil an egg at 9,500 feet as it does at sea level.

- *Pot lid.* Food cooks faster in a covered pot.

- *Amount of fuel.* A full fuel tank works more efficiently than a tank that is almost empty.

- *Oxygen.* At high altitudes, lack of oxygen and lower air pressure reduce fuel performance.

- *Temperature.* Below-freezing temperatures reduce the efficiency of butane stoves. In cold weather, insulate the stove from the cold ground by using closed cell foam insulation under the base of the stove. (Closed cell foam can be obtained from a camping supply store.)

- *Wind.* Wind can cool the cooking pot and blow the flame away from the pot, which increases cooking time. Use the wind shield provided by the stove manufacturer and create additional wind shields around the stove when necessary.

- *Type of food.* Foods that simply require the addition of hot water are faster to prepare and also use less fuel than foods that require long cooking. Large pieces of food take longer to cook than smaller pieces.

- *Distance between flame and pot.* The closer the flame to the pot, the faster the food will cook.

- *Size of flame.* The size of the flame should match the size of the pot.

- *Heat of flame.* The hotter the flame, the more rapidly food will cook. A flame appears blue to white when it is hottest and red when it is coolest.

Stove Safety

Always read and follow stove instructions carefully before operating. The following safety precautions must be taken:

- Test the stove and become familiar with its operation before using it on a trip.

- Anyone operating the stove must learn to use it properly and safely. An adult must be present to supervise the use of any stove while girls are cooking.

- Practice replacing parts before taking the stove on a camping trip. Know the proper tools to use.

- When replacing parts of a stove, make sure the parts are correct and approved by the manufacturer.

- Keep all stove parts clean and see that connecting lines and burners are not clogged. Make sure all rubber or plastic lines are not cracked or cut. Maintain the stove according to the manufacturer's instructions.

- To avoid an accident, a stove must be used on a level surface and out of the way of foot traffic.

- A liquid fuel stove should not be refueled in the cooking area. Carry the stove away from any flammable equipment and the cooking area before refueling it.

- Refuel the stove on a level surface after it has cooled down.

- When using liquid fuels, use a funnel to transfer the fuel from the container to the stove.

- No flame should be present in any site where fuel may have spilled.

- **Never** open a refillable fuel tank while the stove is ignited, even if the tank is running low.

- To avoid a flare-up when lighting the stove, do not overfill it.

- For stoves that require priming, be careful to avoid over-priming and spilling fuel.

- If the stove has a refillable tank, before each meal make sure that the tank has enough fuel to cook the meal.

- Liquid fuel must be carried in a clearly marked bottle with a tight-fitting gasket. Avoid contamination of food or spillage on clothing by carrying the stove and fuel upright in plastic bags separated from food and clothing.

- If a fuel canister is used and emptied on the trip, carry it out for proper refilling or disposal.

- When using butane or propane, be sure to carefully thread the canisters to the stove coupling so there is no leakage. Test the coupling with a soap solution. If bubbles form, reconnect the coupling carefully to make a tight fit.

- **Never** put an empty fuel canister in a fire; it will explode!

- **Never** cook inside a tent. The risk of a fire is too great and a stove gives off carbon monoxide gas, which is deadly and cannot be smelled. Even in bad weather, cook outdoors.

- Always make certain that the cooking utensils are appropriate to the type and size of the stove. Never use pots that make the stove top-heavy.

- Concentrate the heat under the pot by using a windscreen. Be sure there is proper ventilation for the flame and the fuel tank.

- Never leave a lighted stove unattended.

- In preparation for working near any open flame, tie back long hair, roll up loose sleeves, and do not wear clothing with dangling ends. Plastic or synthetic garments are extremely flammable and can cause severe burns, as they often melt rather than burn. Clothes made of natural fibers are much safer.

Charcoal Fires

A ready-made charcoal grill in a park or backyard is designed to enhance air flow. Charcoal is also used as the fuel in box ovens, which girls can enjoy using to bake many things from cookies to pizza.

A charcoal stove for one person can be made from a large tin can. The stove is designed so that a draft of air flows past the charcoal.

Activity Suggestion

Tin Can Charcoal Stove

Materials:

Tin can, #10 or larger
2 pieces of sturdy wire screen
Roll-type can opener
3 or 4 charcoal briquettes
Punch-type can opener
Wire for handle

1. Remove the top of the can with a can opener. Punch air holes with a can opener around the top and bottom of the can. The bottom holes are the openings through which the stove should be lit.

2. Push the ends of the wire through two of the holes at the top and twist to make a handle. This handle is convenient when it is time to pack up, but beware of the hot handle when cooking.

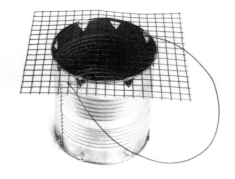

Tin can charcoal stove.

3. Push one piece of wire screen halfway down into the can to make a grate. This holds charcoal near the top for cooking and provides air space under the charcoal.

4. Make a stove top out of the second piece of wire screen. This supports the pot.

Preparing the fire. Set the stove on cleared ground. Fire starters are necessary to ignite charcoal (see next page). Put fire starters on the wire screen inside the can. Carefully pile charcoal around the fire starters to allow proper air flow. It takes about half an hour for a charcoal fire to reach the ember stage (gray coals) for cooking.

Fire Starters

Whenever a trip will include using charcoal, a few minutes spent making fire starters will be a great help. Fire starters are highly flammable materials that ignite at the touch of a match. The simplest fire starters are stubs of candles, twists of a paper napkin, or newspaper. Commercial fire starters may be purchased. Two types of fire starters that can be made in advance are "egg" fire starters and trench candles.

Firestarters made from cardboard egg cartons, sawdust, and melted paraffin.

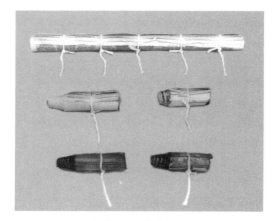

Firestarters made from rolled newspaper dipped in paraffin.

Activity Suggestion

"Egg" Fire Starters

1. Fill cardboard egg carton compartments halfway with sawdust, lint, or wood shavings. Then pour melted paraffin or candle ends into each compartment until each space is full. (Wax should be melted in a double boiler and poured with adult supervision.)

2. When cool, break apart each "egg" or store the whole carton for future use. Then place one "egg" in the kindling and light a match.

Activity Suggestion

Trench Candles

1. Roll several sheets of newspaper into a long, tight roll. Then tie the roll with string at 2 1/2-inch intervals. Leave an 8-inch end on each string to hold while dipping.

2. Cut the roll between the strings.

3. Dip each trench candle into a container of melted wax. Then hang the trench candles by the strings to dry.

Extinguishing a charcoal fire. When the cooking is done, carefully sprinkle water over each piece of charcoal. Charcoal must be well soaked with water before you can consider it extinguished. Lay charcoal out to dry for reuse. Then, put the charcoal in a metal container with a tight cover and take it with you.

If the charcoal will not be reused, make sure to soak the charcoal and crush each piece with a rock. When the charcoal is completely cool to the touch, shovel it into the garbage for disposal. Do not dispose of charcoal in the woods.

Solar Cooking

In areas that receive a great deal of sunshine, solar cookers are practical and make excellent use of a free energy

This solar box cooker, a 2 feet by 2 ½ feet by 1 foot insulated cardboard container, has aluminum foil lining the inside, a glass top, and a reflective lid. The materials are inexpensive, and it only takes a few hours to assemble.

source. Instructions for making one type of solar cooker are given in the *Brownie Girl Scout Handbook*, pages 197–198, and in *Girl Scout Badges and Signs*, pages 242–243.

Activity Suggestion

Making a Solar Box Cooker

A solar box cooker should have a window of about 400 square inches for patrol-size groups. Generally a square foot of window can cook about five pounds of food. The outer sides and bottoms of pots and pans should be a dark color or painted black. All pots should be covered with a dark-colored, tight-fitting lid. In most regions of the United States, a solar cooker can be used for six to eight months of the year. Choose a spot that will be in sunlight for several hours. Midday is the best cooking time. Cooking time is longer with large amounts of food, if the sky is partly cloudy, or when the sun is low in the sky. Once the food is prepared and placed in the cooker, it can be left all day. Other program activities can take place until it is time to eat.

Observe the following safety precautions when using a solar box cooker:

- Always use potholders when removing pots from the solar oven.

- Be careful of escaping hot steam when removing the lid from the box and the lid from the pot after cooking.

A solar cooker made from pieces of corrugated cardboard covered with aluminum foil. The pot in the center is painted with dull black paint and inserted into a plastic bag for cooking.

- Put an oven thermometer at the back edge of the bottom of the oven to remind users how hot the oven is.

- When it is not in use, close the lid of the solar oven.

Wood Fires

Wood fires may be used in the following circumstances: where burning wood is permitted, when the danger of fire is low, or in emergencies for cooking, warmth, or signaling. Check local fire ordinances and find out if there are any air pollution regulations to consider. Check the local weather conditions. Make sure it is not too dry or windy for a safe fire.

The three basic elements for a fire are fuel, flame (or intense heat), and air (oxygen). To build a wood fire, use three different sizes of wood—tinder, kindling, and fuel.

Tinder is any small piece of natural material that burns as soon as it is touched with a match. It can be dry wood, dried leaves, wood shavings, dried pine needles or cones, bark from a dead tree, or paper twisted into spirals.

Kindling is larger in diameter than tinder, but generally smaller than the diameter of an adult's thumb. It must be thin enough to catch fire quickly before the tinder burns out, but large enough to ignite larger fuel. Twigs or splintered pieces of wood can be used for kindling. Both tinder and kindling should be as dry as possible to catch fire quickly. To test dryness, see if the wood snaps, rather than bends, when broken.

Fuel is the larger wood that keeps a fire going. Fuel might be charcoal or might be dry, seasoned wood found on the ground. At some sites, it may be necessary to bring in wood for fuel or buy it.

The different sizes of wood, from left to right: tinder, kindling, and fuel.

When building a fire, consider the type of wood to be used. Hardwoods, such as oak, hickory, birch, maple, ash, eucalyptus, and mesquite, produce a long-burning fire with lasting coals. Softwoods, such as pine, spruce, cedar, gray birch, and aspen, produce a quick, hot fire and provide excellent fuel for starting a long-burning fire with harder wood.

At high-use campsites, fires should always be built in established fire circles or in a spot where fires have been constructed previously. Fires should not be built on soil containing decaying leaves or roots. Be aware that fires can travel underground by burning along roots or traveling through highly organic materials in the soil. The fire can pop back to the surface many feet from the original fire site and many hours later, often after campers have left the site. If a new fire site must be built, this should be done on mineral soil to minimize the chance that the fire will unintentionally spread.

Always have a large bucket of water or sand near the fire before striking the first match. Once the precautions outlined above have been considered, follow these three steps to build a fire:

1. Make a small triangle with three pieces of kindling. Leave an air space under the top bar of the triangle. Lay a handful of tinder upright against the top stick. (A fire starter may be used in place of tinder.)

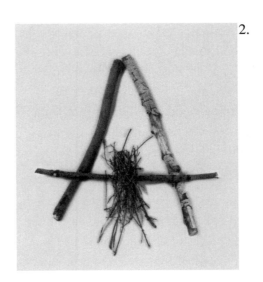
2.

Strike the match close to the wood. Hold the match beneath the tinder until the flame burns up through the tinder, then place additional tinder and kindling onto the fire. Place each piece of kindling separately. Remember to have enough extra tinder, kindling, and fuel within close reach.

3. Fires need oxygen to burn. Arrange the wood so that a small space lies between the pieces. Place the pieces of wood close enough so that one piece of burning wood will light the adjoining pieces. Once the kindling is burning, add fuel. Use just enough fuel for cooking needs.

If heat needs to be concentrated—under a pot to boil water, for example—continue to add pieces of kindling to the fire to form a cone. If food needs to be cooked for a longer period of time, add more kindling and then fuel to the fire. As the fuel burns down, the bed of coals that is formed will provide a more even, long-lasting heat source.

When the need for a fire is finished:

- Burn remaining wood to ash and let the fire die down. Grind any remaining charcoal to powder.

- Stir the ashes, sprinkle them with water, then stir them again. Repeat until there is no gray ash anywhere in the fire pit. (Do not pour water on a fireplace. The water may cause the stones to crack.)

- A hand passed several inches above the ashes will indicate whether or not the spot is still hot. Sprinkle hot spots with more water. Then hold a steady hand several inches above the ashes. Finally, when a hand can be pressed on the spot where the fire was and not feel any warmth, the fire is out.

- Scatter the ashes a distance from the campsite and over a wide area so no signs of ashes remain.

- A firepit constructed by the group should be filled in with soil and then with sod or leaf litter to give the appearance that the earth has not been disturbed. No trace of a fire should remain.

When one of the modern portable stoves described in this chapter is used, cooking meals will take far less time than is needed to cook over wood fires. Solar cooking is an excellent alternative, since the group can prepare an evening meal right after breakfast, set up the solar oven, and leave the food to cook all day while the girls enjoy outdoor activities. A wide variety of tasty recipes are available to use with groups of different sizes (see the "Camping" section of the Bibliography).

Chapter 4

Let's Go Camping

Girl Scout camping is an experience that provides a creative, educational opportunity in group living in the outdoors. Its purpose is to utilize Girl Scout program, trained leadership, and the resources of the natural surroundings to contribute to each camper's mental, physical, social, and spiritual growth. For many girls, camping is a highlight of Girl Scouting. Outdoor experiences and challenges become prized memories.

However, camping techniques and ethics have changed dramatically since Juliette Low first took girls on an overnight adventure along the Savannah River. In the early days of camping, the wilderness was conquered with little thought about human impact on the natural environment. Trees were cut for firewood, large cooking fires were built, the soil on trails was compacted and eroded by humans and livestock, campsites were overused, and large, deep group latrines were dug for human waste.

Introducing Minimal Impact Outdoor Skills

Today, Girl Scouts of all ages learn and practice minimal impact outdoor skills, a method that encourages each person to live lightly on the land and leave no trace of her presence after a trip or activity. Many outdoor recreational activities have become so popular with the American public that our favorite natural areas are being loved to death. Minimal impact skills require each of us to adopt a code of behavior that reflects a commitment to preserving the natural quality of our lands. This means that we understand the philosophy behind the skills so that we can adapt them as the situation changes in different environments and conditions. As groups move through a progressive series of trips from backyard cookouts, to

overnights at Girl Scout program centers, to hikes in local and state parks, to trips into backcountry and wilderness areas, the need for minimal impact skills and knowledge about those skills grows. Minimal impact camping requires advance planning for a trip as well as on-the-spot action. Through these experiences, girls will also understand how they can apply these skills in the future when camping, hiking, or canoeing with family and friends. New attitudes, approaches, skills, and equipment are necessary to ensure that all Americans help to protect the natural environment for future generations.

Girls can begin to discover the beauty of the outdoors and can become comfortable in the natural environment by engaging in activities in their own neighborhoods (see Chapter 2). Some of the concepts of a minimal impact camping approach may be taught before girls go camping. Girls need to understand that their daily actions have an effect on the environment. Each girl can learn and practice simple activities that will lead to an understanding and application of minimal impact camping skills.

At troop meetings each girl should be responsible for cleaning up after herself, not wasting materials, turning off unnecessary lights, conserving water, and leaving the meeting place cleaner than she found it.

When girls move from an indoor setting to the outdoors, help them practice additional skills. Each girl should:

- Learn how to work with others in a group setting by setting goals and planning and carrying out activities together.

- Learn how to dress properly for different kinds of weather.

- Experience a variety of outdoor activities, such as a hike, backyard sleepout, or nature walk.

- Learn about the environment by using the senses—for example, looking at plants, watching birds and animals.

- Learn safety rules for outdoor activities.

- Learn to read a map to get where she wants to go.

- Try some simple food preparation.

The First Overnight Trip

Overnight experiences away from home can be important to the development of girls because they provide a "laboratory experience in life" where girls get to test themselves in new but safe circumstances— ones for which they have planned and prepared. Girls grow as a result because these activities:

- Enhance trust among girls as they build friendships and teamwork skills.

- Build self-confidence.

- Expand horizons as girls live and work in a new environment.

- Build bonds between adults and girls.

- Provide opportunities for girls to increase their skills and feel good about their accomplishments.

The first night away from home on a Girl Scout overnight is a big step and a real adventure, especially for younger girls. A girl needs to be emotionally ready for this experience and should have a genuine desire to go, whether the girls are sleeping overnight in a backyard, joining a museum camp-in, staying in a lodge or cabin, or trying out tent camping. The skills that are necessary to make each girl's experience more enjoyable can be developed through activities at the troop meeting and during progressive short trips with the troop. Some girls may also have skills gained while camping or traveling with the family.

Consider these guidelines for a girl's first overnight:

- She should want to go.

- She should not be afraid to be away from her home or family overnight (and her family should be prepared to let her go).

- She should be able to cope with new circumstances such as:
  —meeting new people
  —visiting strange places
  —darkness (no electricity or night light), different night noises, insects, and other small creatures
  —sleeping in a strange bed or on a pad on the floor

- She can function as a member of a group.

- She is willing to sleep, eat, and play with all girls, not just her best friends.

- She can be flexible, not always have her own way.

- She can share her space and manage with little privacy.

The following indicators can be used as a guide in determining whether or not a girl possesses the necessary skills and knowledge to enjoy an overnight experience and can work cooperatively with other girls.

- She can participate in planning a simple trip; use a kaper chart or similar assignment sheet; and follow written, verbal, or illustrated instructions for food preparation.

- She can wash dishes, clean up the kitchen/cooking area, and store food properly.

- She has practiced packing and repacking her luggage, rolling her bedroll or sleeping bag, using a flashlight, etc.

- She has been on a series of day trips, has participated in cookouts, or has gone on a backyard or family camping overnight.

Be sure that directions have been adapted for girls who find reading print difficult. Simplified verbal instruction, audiotapes, or illustrations may be helpful.

The girls as a group must also be ready for an overnight experience. Their ability to work together, plan together, and play together will help to make the experience a good one for everyone.

The leader of the group must also be ready to guide the planning process, to help everyone feel prepared for and excited about a new adventure. Girl Scout councils provide training for the adults to prepare for this role. There are also a number of resources to help guide the process. The handbooks for each age level provide many suggestions for outdoor activities. Brownie Girl Scout Try-its, Junior Girl Scout badges, and interest projects for Cadette and Senior Girl Scouts are designed to lead girls through progressive outdoor experiences. Girls and leaders can use them to guide their planning whether or not the girls complete and earn the recognitions. See the chart on pages 10–13.

What Type of Overnight?

Once girls are ready to go on an overnight or camping trip, the troop or group must decide what type of experience will meet its readiness level. Usually, younger girls camp in lodges, cabins, or platform tents at established Girl Scout sites. Older, more experienced campers may choose a more challenging type of camping such as backpacking, horse packing, or canoe tripping. (Planning more advanced trips is discussed in Chapter 8.) The following information should be considered at all skill levels.

Where to Go?

After the type of camping has been chosen, the troop or group will need to select a camping location. This may be accomplished by checking with:

- Your Girl Scout council.

- Town or county parks department.

- Other youth-serving agencies.

- Private campgrounds.

- Youth hostels.

- Conference center.

- State park system.

- National parks, national forests, or Bureau of Land Management sites.

- *Trekking Network Directory* provided to Girl Scout councils by GSUSA.

For the sites that may be used, find out:

- Location, distance from home in miles and time.

- Facilities available, capacity for girls and adults.

- Dates available.

- Cost for expected use.

- Type of food preparation area, stove, refrigeration.

- Type of restroom facilities, showers.

- Safe water supply.

- Nearby emergency services, hospital, doctor on call.

- Distance from parking to camping area.

- Program possibilities.

- Equipment available, free or for rent.

- Accessibility of the site and activities for participants with disabilities.

If possible, visit and take a tour of the site chosen, or talk with someone who has taken a group there, to determine what the group will need to bring and what program possibilities are available.

An adult, trained by the council to prepare a group for an overnight, must work with the group in preparation for the trip. Use *Safety-Wise* to determine the number of adults needed to accompany the group.

During a series of meetings, the group will then plan:

- A budget for the trip.

- Transportation to and from the site.

- Special health and safety considerations.

- Group and personal equipment lists.

- Menus for meals and snacks; shopping lists.

- Arrangements for the packing and storage of food (for example, whether perishable items can be taken and stored safely or whether other alternatives must be chosen).

- Girl Scout program activities that will be fun.

- Provisions for emergencies.

- Any extra insurance necessary.

Choosing Activities

As a troop or group begins to plan an overnight or camping weekend, help girls think about the many activities they could plan and then choose those that are most important to do this time. They can establish mealtimes, set rules for bedtime, and put together a schedule of activities.

Weekend Schedule for Troop 120

Friday	4:00 p.m.	Pack cars and leave school
	5:30 p.m.	Arrive at campsite
	6:00 p.m.	Eat supper and move into unit
	7:30 p.m.	Site orientation and practice fire drill
	8:30 p.m.	Singing, night sounds, and snack
	10:00 p.m.	Bedtime
Saturday	7:30 a.m.	Rise and shine!
	8:30 a.m.	Breakfast and unit cleanup
	10:00 a.m.	Soccer game with Troop 541
	12:00	Lunch
	1 :30 p.m.	Nature hike around pond
	3:00 p.m.	Make and fly kites
	4:00 p.m.	Service project for site
	5:30 p.m.	Dinner
	7:00 p.m.	Rehearse skits
	7:30 p.m.	Skits, charades, and songs
	9:00 p.m.	Sky search, snack
	10:00 p.m.	Bedtime
Sunday	7:30 a.m.	Rise and shine!
	8:30 a.m.	Breakfast
	9:30 a.m.	Pack belongings
	10:30 a.m.	Girl Scouts' Own ceremony
	11:30 a.m.	Depart for home

4

Here are some program possibilities to share with the group of girls if they need help in choosing activities.

join in a wide game

do a flag ceremony

plan and do a Girl Scouts' Own ceremony

teach or play a game

act in a skit

do charades

work on a badge activity

go for a hike

row a boat/paddle a canoe

prepare a meal

share a meal or activity with another troop

use a magnifying lens

learn to use binoculars

go swimming at a supervised waterfront

do water tests on a local water source

look at a drop of pond water under a magnifier

make a collage

invent an animal using found objects

weave a wall hanging (include twigs and grasses)

construct a mobile

practice a craft

learn to find constellations

look for craters on the moon

learn first aid

learn songs and enjoy singing them with others

plan a surprise that will be fun for members of your group or another group using the same site

find
  plants
  with
  different
  leaf shapes

make rubbings of things with interesting textures

explore to see what plants, animals, and birds live on the site

have a patrol meeting

listen quietly for three minutes and compare with others the sounds heard

listen for night sounds

listen to the sounds of a wind or rain storm

sketch something in nature

play a sport appropriate to the site

dip a net into a pond and find out what lives there

find out the location of poison ivy or other plants to avoid

write a poem or short story

watch a flying insect such as a dragonfly or butterfly

find a flower blooming

make a sundial

make sun tea or jam

take a hike to find colors in nature

watch a rainbow

find a safe place to go in a storm

hold a practice fire drill

find several kinds of seeds and figure out how they move to new locations

find a feather and look at it with a magnifying lens

study a tree stump; count the rings

find a tree that is like an apartment
  building; discover what lives there

find out what lives in a rotting log

write thank-you notes to troop
  helpers like drivers and shoppers

design a patrol flag

make a box oven and use it

have a party around a theme
  of a favorite story or
  character

fly a kite

sing, dance,
  play instruments

make rhythm instruments

Nighttime

plan a program for a small
  campfire

do skits or create shadow figures

look for insects attracted to lights

do an outdoor search to find what makes
  sounds at night

watch for animals active at night
  (like bats)

go on a night hike using red plastic over
  the flashlight

look for constellations; tell stories about
  the stars

hold a night watch and record the things
  seen and heard during the night

Rain/Inclement Weather

dress appropriately and go out for a short
  activity to enjoy it!

write a group log

give a puppet show using available
  materials (socks, mittens)

practice first aid

do skits, charades

play a game

review how to tie knots,
  learn new ones

start a journal

start a discussion on
  a topic of interest to
  the group

Kaper Charts

The jobs that need to be done while on an overnight, such as cooking, setting the table, and cleaning up, are called kapers and may be listed on a kaper chart. The kaper chart is usually drawn up before the trip so that everyone knows which jobs need to be done and who will do them.

The easiest way to divide up the jobs is for the girls to work together as patrols, pairs, or committees. Jobs can be rotated among the patrols so that everyone has a chance to do each of the different jobs.

Below is an example of a group kaper chart.

	MEAL PREPARERS	DISHWASHERS	TABLE SETTERS AND RECYCLERS
SAT. BREAKFAST	allison Janine Rebecca	Angela Kenya Robyn	Amanda christine Stephanie
SAT. LUNCH	Amanda christine Stephanie	allison Janine Rebecca	angela Kenya Robyn
SAT. DINNER	christine Janine Kenya	Rebecca Robyn Stephanie	allison Amanda angela
SUN. BREAKFAST	Rebecca Robyn Stephanie	allison amanda angela	Christine Janine Kenya

Equipment for Outdoor Trips

For beginners, choose a site with shelter, such as a lodge or cabin, whenever possible. Determine what equipment is available at the site that can be used by the group. The checklist in the Appendix will help. If you are using a Girl Scout council facility, a complete list of equipment available on the site should be available to the troop. Bring along only those items necessary. Plan time to acquaint each person with the equipment she may be using.

For more adventurous trips, purchasing or borrowing the proper equipment for an outdoor experience may require careful research and investigation. (See Chapter 9 for more information on choosing equipment for backcountry trips.) Many Girl Scout councils maintain an equipment bank from which troops may borrow. Check with your council. Some outdoor stores also rent equipment to groups.

There is a wide selection of equipment today for almost every outdoor activity, and the range of quality and expense varies greatly. The equipment selected must be suitable for the age, size, experience, and ability of the individual. Backpacks, for example, must be adjusted and sized to fit each individual. Safety helmets must be rated for the particular activity and must fit properly. Each person must have equipment that is comfortable for her. (See *Safety-Wise*,

pages 54–124, for further guidelines on safety equipment that is needed for particular activities.) Safety equipment must be used or be easily accessible.

Whether owned, borrowed, or rented, equipment must be in good condition. Any equipment that appears defective must never be used and must be marked for repair or disposal. A safety check of equipment must be conducted prior to an activity.

The manufacturer's instructions for safe use and care of equipment must be read and observed prior to using any equipment. In some cases, girls' lives may depend on the quality of the equipment and the way it is used.

Personal Equipment for Each Participant

Discuss with all the participants which items will be needed for the expected weather and activities as well as for changes in weather that could occur. (The same item of clothing can also serve several purposes, such as socks to keep feet and hands warm.) Provide a list for each girl and adult to take home to use as a checklist for packing. If this is the first trip, parents/guardians may need an orientation to understand what types of items are needed. Others will need help finding items that can be borrowed for the trip (see Appendix).

Girls can make a bedroll using a sheet of plastic (or a poncho), a single bed sheet, and several blankets, depending on the weather. The plastic sheet makes a good outside layer to keep the blankets clean and dry during packing and traveling.

1

Lay out a plastic sheet on the floor and then place blankets on top, overlapping each by half. Lay a folded sheet on top. Then fold blanket A, then B, then C over the sheet to create an envelope for sleeping.

2

The bottom edge and side can be pinned together with large pins to hold the bedroll together. Complete by folding over the plastic sheet.

3

Roll it up and tie with sturdy cord.

Girls may wish to buy a sleeping bag. For girls who have never camped before or are trying out a new type of outdoor trip, selecting the right sleeping bag is a big decision, but it can mean the difference between a good night's rest and sheer misery and discomfort. No one sleeping bag can address the requirements for all outdoor adventures, but one can be borrowed or purchased that will meet a wide array of needs. Be sure to try out any bag to see if the fit is right. In selecting a sleeping bag, check with an experienced camper or knowledgeable salesperson and consider the following factors.

- Will the sleeping bag be used by an adult or a child?

- Does she usually feel warm or cold while sleeping?

- What shape, size, and weight of sleeping bag will be comfortable?

- What are the expected overnight temperatures at the time(s) of year when the sleeping bag will be used?

- What type of trip is planned? Cabin camping? Backpacking in cooler weather in the mountains? A canoe trip? Car camping?

- Where is the trip planned? A desert? An area that typically receives a lot of moisture? A heated facility?

Shape. Sleeping bags come in several styles and shapes:

Mummy bags are narrow at the feet, wider at the shoulders, and have a hood. There is usually a top-to-bottom zipper along one side. The narrow shape reduces the weight when carrying it, but some people feel claustrophobic in the tight confines of this type of bag. Body heat warms the inside of the bag efficiently.

Rectangular bags have sufficient room to move around and have a top-to-bottom zipper along one side. There is a lot more space in the interior to heat and a loss of warmth around the neck and shoulders. This type of sleeping bag is often used for car or cabin camping where the weight of carrying it is not a problem.

Semi-rectangular bags incorporate the top-to-bottom zipper and room-to-roll features of a rectangular bag, but are more tapered and are usually warmer than a rectangular bag. Some bags have a drawstring at the shoulder level to help retain heat.

Size. Sleeping bags come in varying sizes: child, regular, large, and oversized. Select a sleeping bag that has enough material for the individual to lie flat comfortably, but not too much extra room in length or width to heat. Some people may wish to allow a little extra space for a sleeping bag liner. Girls may not be comfortable in a sleeping bag designed for a large adult. A small girl does not have the body heat to warm up a big sleeping bag. She will be cold all night and poorly rested the next morning. Choose a sleeping bag specifically sized for a child.

Mummy-shape sleeping bag.

Rectangular sleeping bag.

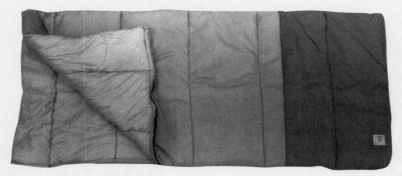

Semi-rectangular sleeping bag.

Child-size sleeping bag.

Fills. For many years, sleeping bags were only filled with down feathers. Down is lightweight, warm, and stuffs easily into a small sack. The biggest disadvantage of down is that it becomes a soggy, useless clump of feathers when wet. Down bags also require extreme care in storing and washing in order to retain their loft.

Today, in addition to down, there are a number of synthetic fiber fills used in sleeping bags which are less expensive than down, will insulate even when wet, are machine washable, dry fairly rapidly, and are hypoallergenic. The newest synthetic fibers on the market are similar to down in weight, stay warm when wet, and are compressible. Synthetic materials are a good choice for a bag to be used by a child. Older girls can better understand the care needed when using a down bag.

Temperature ratings. When buying a sleeping bag, check the manufacturer's recommendations for the lowest temperatures at which the bag can comfortably be used. A sleeping bag rated as suitable for three seasons will be sufficient, unless the camping trip is in an extremely hot region that does not cool off at night or unless a winter camping trip is planned for very cold conditions. There is no formula for selecting a sleeping bag that will always be comfortable for an individual. Consider carefully when and where the sleeping bag

will be used. To be safe, use a bag rated for 10 degrees F below the coldest anticipated temperature. The size of the bag and other considerations noted in this section also add to comfort when sleeping outdoors.

Sleeping comfortably. Just as at home, the sleeping environment can be regulated. Put on clean and dry sleepwear. In cold weather, before bedtime, lay out the bedroll or sleeping bag and shake it to give it loft. Warmth comes from the air trapped inside the insulation. The greater the loft, the warmer the person will be. Use an insulating pad under the sleeping bag or bedroll. Don't go to bed chilled. Have a hot drink before going to sleep. For extra warmth, zip up the tent and wear a ski cap or use the hood or drawstring on the sleeping bag, if there is one. In warm weather, unzip the sleeping bag partially or all the way and adjust the zipper throughout the night. A camper may even choose to use the sleeping bag as a comforter or sleep on the bag and put a sheet or sleeping bag liner over herself.

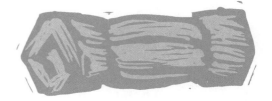

Setting Up a Campsite

When the group plans to camp at an established campsite, cooking and living areas may already be designated. These should be utilized in order to minimize the impact of activities on the rest of the site. Carefully store food to keep it fresh and away from animals. Check restrooms for supplies and cleanliness. If camping in tents, the adults in charge should choose a tent in a central location so that they can supervise the area and be accessible to girls who need to find them. Designate places for the first aid kit and other emergency supplies. Tour the site to find the location of various features and equipment and establish fire drill and other procedures.

Platform Tents

Many Girl Scout councils provide large tents on wooden platforms for troops/groups to use. It is important that girls understand how to take care of platform tents.

- Never use a heater or any open flame in or near a tent.

- The guy ropes along the sides may need to be loosened in rain. When they are wet, they tighten and put undue strain on the canvas.

- Do not hang anything on the ropes. This pulls the tent out of line.

- Roll side walls and door flaps up toward the inside of the tent, so they can be let down from the inside. This prevents water from catching in the roll when it rains.

- Never roll up the side walls or door flaps unless they are completely dry. Damp canvas will mildew when not open to the air.

- Drop the side walls periodically. Mice sometimes nest in the rolled-up flaps.

- Never touch the inside of the tent during a rain. Touching the fabric can cause the canvas to leak.

- Do not use insect sprays or other kinds of sprays inside a tent. The chemicals can dissolve the water-repellent treatment.

- Do not pin anything to the tent, since this can cause tears and leaking.

- Tie the tapes with a half bow so they can be untied when wet.

- Keep mirrors under cover. Sunlight reflected in a mirror can be hot enough to burn a hole in a tent or start a fire.

- Report small tears and missing ropes or tapes so that they can be replaced.

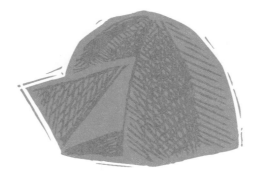

Personal Hygiene and Sanitation

Good health habits are particularly important when camping. Remind girls to brush their teeth, wash their hands and face, and shower or wash with a cloth or bandanna. Some girls may need personal assistance with these tasks.

Handwashing

If running tap water is not available, a simple handwashing unit can be made from a plastic jug and a wooden dowel or twig (see photo). Make a small hole near the bottom of the jug. Use the twig or dowel to plug up the hole before the jug is filled with water. Place a bar of biodegradable soap in an old stocking and tie it nearby. (If you remove the bar of soap from its package and let it dry for several days before the trip, it will harden and last longer.) For better water flow, remove the cap from the jug. Hang one of these handwashing units near the latrine and food preparation areas.

Showers

In established sites, use the showers provided. Conserve water and take short showers. Rinse, turn off the shower and lather up, then turn on the shower for the final rinse. If a cleaning service is not provided, include daily cleaning of showers with a disinfectant on the group kaper chart.

Restrooms

If composting or flush toilets or latrines are provided at the site, girls should clean them daily as part of their kapers (unless a cleaning service is provided). Replenish paper supplies, sweep the floor, clean sinks, and disinfect toilet seats.

Clothes Washing

On a camping trip to an established area, bring sufficient clothing so that washing is not necessary. Limited washing may be done by setting up buckets for washing and rinsing. Hang clothes on a line strung away from foot traffic areas. As much as possible, keep the laundry from visually littering the site. If heavier washing of a large quantity of clothing is necessary, schedule time to go to a laundromat.

Handwashing unit. Bar of soap in stocking is tied nearby.

Garbage Disposal

If a garbage pickup service is available, line cans with plastic bags and make sure the cans are tightly covered at all times. Sort out those items that can be recycled. Flatten cans to save space. In all other situations, plan to carry out all trash. Do not burn or bury any garbage. Careful meal planning will minimize the amount of leftover food. All food residue and trash should be put in garbage bags and disposed of properly.

Leaving the Site

The goal of minimal impact camping is to leave no evidence that your group stayed in a particular area. At Girl Scout program centers, or state or private campgrounds, the camping area is already established with permanent structures such as cabins, tent units, picnic tables, latrines, and fire circles or barbecue pits. Girls can leave these areas better than they found them by carefully cleaning sleeping areas, picking up trash indoors and outdoors, depositing trash in designated receptacles or taking it home for disposal, and cleaning fire circles, if a fire was built.

Evaluating the Experience

An evaluation is part of every Girl Scout activity. It is the first step in building future successes. Together, adults and girls should evaluate each phase of the outdoor experience or trip. This allows for changes or adaptations that can improve the total outcome while the activity is still in progress.

The following questions can help focus on the experience and yield valuable information:

- Did the girls have fun? Why or why not?
- Did the adults and girls share in the planning process?
- How was the food?
- How were the sleeping arrangements?
- Did the group have the right equipment?
- What part of the trip was the most fun?
- What part of the trip helped the girls to learn things about themselves?
- Would the girls like to go again?
- What should be changed for the next trip?
- What should stay the same?
- What new skills did the girls learn?
- Did the girls make any new friends?
- Did the girls work on any Girl Scout badge or interest project requirements?

Chapter 5

Staying Safe

Being prepared is the safest and smartest way to prevent accidents and handle emergencies. Safety requires having the right clothing and equipment, doing thorough planning, and being alert to changing conditions and dangers. Girls and leaders can help each other to be alert by using the buddy system.

The Buddy System

Under the buddy system, girls are divided into teams of two. Each person chooses or is assigned a buddy and is responsible for staying with her buddy at all times, warning her buddy of danger, giving her buddy immediate assistance if it is safe to do so, and calling for or going for help when the situation warrants it. The buddy system is one of the most effective methods of protecting girls while they are engaged in outdoor activities or are away from the regular troop meeting place. The buddy system enables a leader to determine quickly the name of a missing person. The system does not relieve the leader of her responsibility for knowing the whereabouts of each member of the group, but it does serve as a means of having each person share responsibility. Leaders need to involve everyone in the buddy system during the pretrip planning, at the beginning of each outing, and during the outing. If the buddy system is to be really effective, all members of the group need to understand how it works and how to adapt the system to each outing or camping trip.

Girls and adults can choose their buddies at the start of the trip or upon arrival at the campsite. If there is an odd number, expand one team to include three members. Review all possible hazards, "do's and don'ts," the emergency signaling system, where adults can be found, and where to go for help. During the trip, leaders or other adults in charge must conduct periodic buddy checks.

When girls with disabilities are participating, make sure they are paired with other girls rather than with adults, if possible. It is important that all girls spend time with their peers.

Planning Tips

Before a day in the outdoors or a camping trip, the following key points can help to ensure a good experience. In preparation for the trip and before departure:

- Learn the location and telephone number of the police station, fire department, rescue squad or ambulance service, and civil defense center; find out the route to the nearest hospital; and obtain any other applicable emergency information.

- Obtain the name and telephone number of the camp's caretaker or owner of the property.

- Request from parents the necessary information and/or equipment for girls who may be asthmatic, diabetic, seizure-prone, or who may have other health impairments requiring attention.

- Prepare a list that includes:

    —the names of girls and adults going on the trip

    —the name of each girl's parent(s)/ guardian(s), complete address, and telephone number

    —a telephone number for the site

    —Girl Scout council emergency information

—a map of the site with any proposed side trips

—the route (and return trip route, if different)

—an approximate timetable for departures and arrivals

—identification of the vehicle staying with the group—i.e., license plate number, make, year, and color of car

- Appoint at least two emergency contact persons at home or at the local Girl Scout council office. In the event of delays or changes in the original itinerary, the leader notifies the emergency contact persons. Parent(s)/ guardian(s) should be instructed to speak with one of the emergency contact persons for any information during the time of the trip.

- Review all safety rules and procedures to be followed on the trip. Skits, role plays, quiz or flash card games, and discussions can be used to alert girls to the safety and security problems that may be encountered at a campsite or en route to the campsite.

- If aquatic activities are planned, check the procedures in *Safety-Wise* for swimming or using small craft. Each aquatic activity must have the proper lifeguards and supervision. In addition, check any local, state, or federal regulations that might be in effect regarding water safety. Water safety training is available from several sources, including the YMCA and the American Red Cross.

Security and Safety Guidelines

Before going on any trip in the outdoors, become familiar with the security and safety guidelines in this section. Know the names, addresses, and telephone numbers of the appropriate persons in the council to contact for guidance on security and safety issues. Review the council guidelines for camping and trips, as well as sections in *Safety-Wise* concerning program standards (see especially standards 3, 14, 18, and 22) and the activity checkpoints.

Both girls and adults should clearly understand the importance of planning for security and safety. Planning should be done as a partnership so that each person is a part of the process. Plans and precautions must be an integral part of the camping experience and should never be regarded lightly. Establish security plans based on general safety precautions and

on security features and concerns related to the particular campsite. Every person must know where to go and how to act when confronted with an unsafe situation.

Although many security measures remain constant regardless of the outdoor activity or location, some security precautions at an established Girl Scout campsite, public recreation area, or private campsite will differ from camping in the backcountry. With the help of your council, establish a camping security plan.

Security and Safety Rules: Camping at Girl Scout Program Centers

Discuss with the group the following ways for girls to stay safe:

- Use the buddy system at all times.

- Stay near the group. Don't wander from the designated camping area. Girls should be shown the procedures to follow if buddies become separated from the group or one of them gets lost.

- Avoid contact with strangers.

- Sound an alarm, or whistle or scream, when in trouble.

- When feeling threatened or in trouble, move away from the threat and toward people and lights.

- Always carry a flashlight at night. Girls should be told where they can find the adults during daytime as well as at night.

- Report suspicious sounds, activities, or people to the group leader.

- Practice what to do when an alarm sounds at the site. The alarm may be a bell, an air horn, a siren, flashing lights, or a whistle. Flashing lights or some other obvious visual signal is needed for girls who are deaf or hearing-impaired.

Additional Rules: Camping at a Public Campsite or on Private Property

Add the following procedures when camping at a public site or at any site that is not operated by a Girl Scout council:

- Inform law enforcement officials in advance that the group will be camping in a certain area. Ask officials to include the group's campsite in their patrol.

- Find out what kind of alarm system is used at the site in case of emergency.

- Check for a perimeter security system such as a fence or light to define the boundaries of the camping area.

- Set up tents within sight of each other. Tents should not be located too close to roads or boundaries.

- Lock equipment in a building or car when the group is away from the campsite. Or, have an adult stay at the campsite while the group is engaged in activities such as swimming or hiking.

Staying Found

Everyone should safeguard against the possibility of getting lost. Each person should carry a whistle at all times. Three blasts of a whistle (or horn) is a universal distress signal. Girls must understand that the whistle is only to be used in emergency situations. In the event that buddies get lost or separated from the group and become disoriented, the best thing for them to do is *stop* and try not to panic. They should:

- Sit down and evaluate the circumstances.

- Try to determine the last location where they knew where they were.

- Orient themselves to the landscape by using a map (if they have one) or try to recognize familiar landmarks such as large boulders or a fallen tree.

Teach girls that if they locate a familiar landmark they can travel in an ever-widening circular pattern until another familiar landmark is found. They should always keep the last landmark in sight in case there is a need to return to it. Girls should listen carefully for noises, such as traffic or barking dogs, that could lead them to a road. Sounds of moving water can lead to a river. Walking parallel to the river can be another way to reach a road. Make sure there is sufficient daylight to walk to the nearest trail, road, or campsite to obtain help.

If the buddies cannot figure out where they are or where they need to go,

Girls orienting themselves to the landscape by using a map.

moving about will waste energy and will confuse and frighten them even more. In that case, buddies should:

- Sit down and conserve energy. Relax. Try not to panic.

- Find shelter (evergreen grove, rock overhang, a big tree) to keep as warm and dry as possible and out of the wind. Girls should select natural shelter carefully in order to make sure that the shelter is not home to potentially dangerous animals such as bees or poisonous snakes. This can be determined by looking for tracks, scat, scratches in the soil, or other signs that the shelter has been used recently by an animal. If girls decide that the shelter is suitable, they should leave some sort of sign, such as a piece of clothing, outside of the shelter to alert searchers. Otherwise searchers may walk right by the shelter.

- Find water. If at all possible, surface water should be treated before drinking it by boiling, filtering, or using chemical purifiers. In a survival situation, this may not be possible. Water may also be obtained by using a bandanna or cloth to wipe moisture from wet vegetation. Water from the cloth may be wrung out into the mouth.

- If matches are available and the danger of a fire spreading out of control is low, girls may want to build a fire. A fire is comforting and may be used to boil water or to signal for help.

If girls have shelter and water, they can live for many days until they are found. Girls should be taught to consume only plants that they can identify as safe to eat.

Girls should devise as many ways as possible to attract the attention of those searching for them. For example:

- Tie a piece of brightly colored cloth to a high branch or rock.

- Flash a mirror or other reflective surface at any passing aircraft.

- Make a smoky fire in a safe, open place.

- Draw large signs on the ground that could be seen from the air.

- Stay in the area. Don't wander.

- Yell or whistle if someone is heard nearby. (Three blasts on a whistle is a universal distress call.)

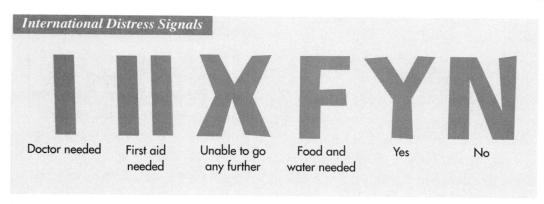

International Distress Signals

I	II	X	F	Y	N
Doctor needed	First aid needed	Unable to go any further	Food and water needed	Yes	No

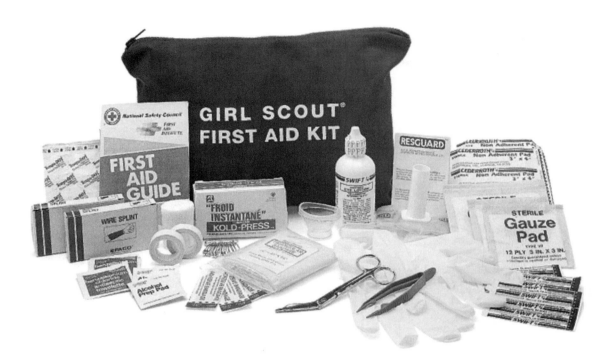

First Aid

First aid is the immediate care given to a person who has been injured or who is suddenly ill. Despite the best safety training and efforts to prevent accidents, situations can occur that require first aid. Medical emergencies may require first aid plus caring for the patient until the individual can be transported to a hospital or help can be summoned.

First Aid Training

Safety-Wise describes the Girl Scout activities that require the presence of a first-aid-trained adult. Leaders should check with their local Girl Scout council for information about the type of first aid training necessary for various activities and when courses are scheduled. First aid training requirements are periodically updated to include new procedures and the types of supplies and equipment currently available. Adults who will be accompanying groups of girls on outdoor activities are urged to take first aid training to learn proper techniques and procedures. It is also helpful for girls to take a first aid course to make them more aware of accident prevention and how they can help in an emergency.

First Aid Kits

Each group should carry a first aid kit adapted to the kinds of activities that will take place during the trip. The contents of the kit will vary according to its intended use and the size of the group.

A group first aid kit is available from NES (Cat. # 5360), or consult a physician for specific recommendations. Whether a commercially made first aid kit is used or the group assembles a kit, it should contain the following items:

Adhesive tape and bandages

Alcohol wipes

Band-Aids, assorted

Bottle of distilled water (for use as an eye rinse or to clean wounds or other items)

Coins for telephone calls

Drinking cups (single-use)

First aid book (see Bibliography)

Flashlight

Gauze pads

Instant chemical ice pack

Latex gloves (disposable, for use in situations involving blood or other body fluids)

List of emergency telephone numbers

Matches (for starting a fire or lighting a stove)

Moleskin and molefoam (for treating blisters and hot spots)

Needle (for removal of splinters or to make a small hole at the base of a blister)

Oral thermometer

Personal care products (sanitary napkins or tampons)

Plastic bags (for disposal of used materials and for collecting vomitus for analysis in suspected oral poisonings)

Single-use pocket face mask or face shield (used in CPR for protection when performing mouth-to-mouth resuscitation)

Roller gauze bandages

Safety pins

Scissors

Soap (antibacterial liquid)

Splints

Triangular bandages

Tweezers

White index card, transparent tape, and self-closing plastic bag (for use when removing objects such as ticks; the item removed can be taped to the index card, enclosed in the plastic bag, and given to a medical professional)

First Aid Cleanup

Latex gloves should be used during any first aid procedure where contact with bodily fluids such as blood may occur. After first aid is given, hands and other skin surfaces that may have come in contact with body fluids should be washed thoroughly with disinfectant and/or antiseptic soap and water. Blood-soaked items, or items that have come in contact with other bodily fluids, should be placed in a leakproof bag until they can be washed (clothing) or thrown away (first aid items). If the group is at an established program site and able to perform a cleanup, wash the items with hot, soapy water while wearing gloves. Reusable equipment, washable floors, furniture, and supplies should be cleaned first with detergent and water and then with a solution of one part chlorine bleach to ten parts of water. Rinse well. If cleaning is not possible during the trip, clean clothing and equipment upon returning home.

First Aid Emergencies

The trained first-aider accompanying a group must be prepared to handle a wide variety of minor cuts, bruises, splinters, and sprains. Depending on the activity and the weather, it may be important to know the symptoms and treatment of the following conditions that can occur during outdoor activities:

Dehydration. During periods of active participation in outdoor activities and sports, it is easy for the body to become dehydrated. Encourage girls to drink water before an activity starts and at breaks along the way. Moisture is lost from the body by breathing as well as perspiration. A lot of moisture is lost even during winter sports or when the humidity is very low and clothes do not become damp from perspiration. Replacing water is essential. Girls should drink as often as possible, not just when they are thirsty.

Signs and symptoms: Fatigue, thirst, irritability, dizziness, headache, lethargy, reduced urine output or dark-colored urine.

First aid: Drink plenty of water to replace what has been lost.

Hypothermia. Hypothermia (lowered body temperature) occurs when the body loses heat faster than it can produce it. This potentially life-threatening situation can develop when wind, moisture, and cool temperatures draw heat away from the body at a rapid rate. Even when the temperature is far above freezing, a dangerous situation can arise. Because of moisture and wind chill, a cool, breezy, drizzly day can be more dangerous in terms of hypothermia than a calm, dry, cold day.

Being prepared is one of the best ways to prevent hypothermia. Stay warm in cold weather by dressing in layers and wearing a hat. Garments made of wool insulate well even when wet. Avoid wearing cotton next to the skin. Cotton holds moisture next to the skin and dries slowly. Prevent getting wet by covering up or immediately changing wet clothes. Eat high-energy foods and drink hot liquids.

Signs and symptoms: Hypothermia progresses from a mild stage (core body temperature above 90 degrees F) to a profound stage (core body temperature below 90 degrees F). Knowing the warning signals can prevent the dangerous progression from mild to profound hypothermia. The mild stage is characterized by:

1. Uncontrollable shivering; cold hands and feet.

2. Clumsiness; loss of dexterity.

3. Loss of reason and recall.

The profound stage is characterized by:

1. Shaking stops; muscles become stiff.

2. Skin looks blue and doesn't react to pain.

3. Pulse and respiration slow; pupils dilate.

4. Collapse.

First aid: For mild hypothermia, gently warm in a warm bath (don't immerse the victim's arms and legs) or use hot towels or blankets, warm air, or body-to-body contact. Seek medical assistance. For profound hypothermia, keep the victim from getting colder and transport immediately to a medical facility. (Death may follow without proper medical assistance.)

HELP position of person in water.

Water immersion hypothermia.
Hypothermia can also occur if a person is in cold water, such as when a boat overturns and the occupant is pitched into the water. Acute exposure takes place when a person loses heat very rapidly. The following techniques can be used to reduce the chances of the onset of hypothermia.

In the event of water immersion, assume the HELP (heat escape lessening position) position to slow cooling from major heat loss areas (groin and sides of chest). The head should be kept out of the water.

Protect the sides of the chest with the arms, cross the ankles to keep the legs together, and, if possible, raise the knees to protect the groin. It's easy to do when sitting on land, but a person needs to be wearing a personal flotation device to hold the position in the water.

The huddle position is used to keep several people warm. To huddle, several people hold each other closely, to preserve body heat.

Huddle position of group.

Frostbite. Frostbite, the most common injury caused by exposure to the cold, is the freezing of parts of the body because of exposure to very low temperatures. Frostbite occurs when ice crystals form in the fluid in the cells of skin and tissues. The nose, cheeks, ears, fingers, and toes are most often affected. Serious frostbite can result in gangrene and may require amputation.

Signs and symptoms:

1. Skin is slightly flushed or reddened.

2. Skin appears gray or white.

3. Pain may be felt early but usually subsides.

4. The affected area feels extremely cold and numb; tingling, stinging, or aching may be felt.

5. When gentle pressure is applied, skin surface feels hard or crusty and the underlying tissue feels soft.

Often, the victim is not aware she has frostbite until someone notices these signs or she observes the pale, glossy skin.

First aid: If medical assistance can be obtained quickly, do not rewarm the affected part. Cover the frozen part with extra clothing or a clean cloth and transport the victim to medical help.

In a situation away from immediate medical help, maintain respiration and protect the frozen area from further injury. Warm the frozen area quickly by following the steps below:

1. Cover the frozen part with extra clothing or a clean cloth.

2. Bring the victim inside promptly.

3. Remove items of clothing or jewelry that could impair blood circulation.

4. Rewarm the frostbitten area rapidly, but gently. Frostbitten tissue is easily damaged, so don't rub the affected parts.

(a) Put the victim's frostbitten part in warm water between 102–105 degrees F. When placed in water, the frostbitten part should not contact the sides or bottom of the water container. Test the water temperature with a thermometer or by pouring water over the inside of your arm. Water should feel warm, not hot.

(b) When it is not possible to immerse the body part (as in the case of ear or facial injuries), place warm, moist cloths on the area. The cloths should be changed often.

(c) If warm water is not available, gently wrap the affected part in a sheet and warm blankets, or in spare articles of clothing.

5. Warming should take 20 to 40 minutes, but should be continued until the tissues feel soft and pliable. Do not break any blisters.

6. Wrap the affected area in loose, clean cloth. If the victim's fingers or toes are involved, place a dry, sterile gauze between them to keep them separated.

7. Elevate the affected part slightly to reduce the pain and swelling.

8. Keep the victim and the affected part warm without overheating.

9. Obtain medical help as soon as possible.

Heat exhaustion. Heat exhaustion can occur after exposure to high temperatures and humidity, or after physical exertion, if fluids are not adequately replaced. Sufficient intake of water is needed to compensate for loss of fluids through sweating. A type of shock occurs because fluid loss causes decreases in blood flow to the vital organs. Heat exhaustion can lead to heatstroke if not treated.

Signs and symptoms:

1. Body temperature is normal or near normal.

2. Skin is cool, pale, and moist.

3. Headache, dizziness, nausea, or vomiting may occur.

4. Pulse is rapid.

5. Pupils are dilated.

6. Muscle cramping or fainting may take place.

7. Urine output is decreased.

First aid:

1. Stop physical exertion and remove the person from the heat to a cooler place.

2. Treat for shock.

3. Remove or loosen the victim's clothing; apply cold packs or wet towels and sheets on the victim's forehead and body.

4. Fan the victim or move her to an air-conditioned room, if available.

5. Replace fluids by giving the victim water to drink if she is conscious. She needs to drink as much as she can tolerate.

6. If there is no improvement in half an hour, seek medical assistance.

Heatstroke (sunstroke). Heatstroke, a disturbance in the body's regulating system, is caused by extremely high body temperatures due to exposure to more heat than the body can manage. Sweating ceases, the body can't cool itself, and body temperature elevates quickly. Heatstroke is a life-threatening emergency. Action must be taken immediately to reduce the victim's body temperature. Knowing the symptoms and first aid procedures on the next page will help you to act quickly.

First aid:

1. Get medical help as soon as possible.

2. Move the victim out of the heat to a cool place.

3. Undress the victim and cool her quickly; immerse her in a cool bath or wrap her in wet towels or sheets and fan her body. (The victim also may be cooled off with a fan or air conditioner, if available.)

4. Continue treatment until body temperature is lowered; then dry the victim.

5. Treat for shock.

Acute mountain sickness. Acute mountain sickness can occur at elevations above 8,000 feet and is brought on by lack of oxygen. It occurs most often in individuals whose bodies have not gradually adjusted to less oxygen at higher elevations.

Elements influencing acute mountain sickness include:

- Speed of ascent—a fast rate increases risk.

- Elevation, especially if camping at a high elevation. At night the rate of breathing decreases, which lowers the amount of oxygen available in the bloodstream.

Signs and symptoms:

1. Victim may be unconscious.

2. Body temperature is extremely high (as much as 106 degrees F)

3. Skin is hot, red, and dry.

4. Pulse is rapid and weak, and respiration is shallow.

- Length of stay at a high elevation—the longer a person remains, the greater the chance for altitude sickness.

- Level of effort—hard work with insufficient fluids or rest time.

- Fluid intake and diet—high fat and protein diets and insufficient fluid intake.

- Vulnerability—some individuals are more prone to acute mountain sickness than others.

Signs and symptoms: Headache, loss of appetite, nausea and vomiting, fluid retention, drowsiness, and decreased urine volume.

First aid: A few days' rest and drinking plenty of fluids may help the individual to acclimatize. If the symptoms persist or the individual worsens, descend 2,000-3,000 feet or to the elevation where the individual first began to feel badly. If she does not feel better, seek medical attention.

Bites and stings. During an outing it is possible to come in contact with a variety of insects, spiders, ticks, and scorpions—depending on the part of the country where the activity takes place. Learn about the creatures typical of the area of your trip and how best to avoid them. Bites and stings are rarely serious unless the person has an allergic reaction to the bite or the pest is carrying a disease that is injected into the person with the bite. Be prepared with appropriate clothing and repellents and know how to avoid being bitten.

If the stinger from a bee, wasp, or hornet remains in the skin, scrape it off while being careful not to squeeze it, which would release more venom into the victim. Apply cold compresses or ice packs and watch for signs of an allergic reaction. The reaction can occur within minutes or take place hours or days later. People who know they have severe reactions generally carry a bee-sting kit. If an allergic reaction occurs, get the person to medical help as soon as possible.

If camping in scorpion territory, be sure to watch where you step, sit, and put your hands, particularly after dark. Shake out shoes and clothing before putting them on.

Be aware of the diseases that may be prevalent in the locality of the trip. Girls should be told not to pick up, pet, or feed wild animals. Rabies and other diseases are increasing problems in many parts of the country.

Tick bites. Ticks in different parts of the country carry a variety of diseases including Rocky Mountain spotted fever and Lyme disease. Ticks carrying Rocky Mountain spotted fever are widely distributed across the country. Remove any embedded tick with fine-pointed tweezers by grasping it very close to the skin and pulling firmly. Wash the area with soap and water and apply alcohol.

Apply a cold pack if the area is painful. Watch for symptoms such as severe headaches, fever, or rash that may develop several days later.

Lyme disease is a bacterial infection that is transmitted by the bite of an infected tick. Ticks infected with Lyme disease are spreading rapidly through several parts of the United States. These areas include coastal portions of Massachusetts, Rhode Island, Connecticut, New York, and New Jersey; portions of Wisconsin and Minnesota in the Midwest; and coastal areas north of San Francisco. The disease has been reported in 45 states.

The disease is carried by different species of ticks in different parts of the country. In the Northeast the very tiny deer tick, or black-legged tick *(Ixodes scapularis)*, is so small that many people may not know that they have been bitten. The western black-legged tick *(Ixodes pacificus)* is the carrier on the West Coast. The lone star tick *(Amblyomma americanum)*, Pacific Coast tick *(D. occidentalis)*, and American dog tick *(Dermacenter variabilis)* are potential carriers in several parts of the country. Girls and adults must learn to recognize the tick.

Ticks are most active and likely to bite people during the months of warm weather. The tick's habitat includes wooded areas and adjacent grassy fields and lawns. Ticks crawl onto their hosts. They do not jump or fly. Deer, mice, and

| Lone star tick (Amblyomma americanum) ¼ inch long | American dog tick (Dermacentor variabilis) ¼ inch long | Pacific Coast tick (D. occidentalis) ¼ inch long | Black-legged tick (Ixodes scapularis) Up to ⅛ inch long | Western black-legged tick (I. pacificus) Up to ⅛ inch long |

birds also serve as hosts and carriers of the disease as the tick seeks out blood meals several times during its life cycle. Cats, dogs, and horses are also susceptible to Lyme disease.

There are three steps for reducing the risk of tick bites.

1. Avoid walking through dense woods and grasses. Stay on pathways and trails. Avoid sitting or lying on grass or on the ground in forested areas.

2. Wear proper clothing. Long, light-colored pants tucked into socks will help in spotting ticks before they bite. A tucked-in shirt with snug collar and cuffs may also help. Tick repellents containing less than 30 percent DEET should be applied to the clothing of adults. Children should use a tick repellent with less than 20 percent DEET. Products containing Permanone are also highly effective against ticks. These products are applied to clothing before dressing and should not be applied to the skin.

3. Each person must monitor herself. Inspect clothing and body after being outdoors. Help others check areas that are hard for an individual to see, such as hair and the area behind the knee. Shower and shampoo after being outdoors.

Signs and symptoms: Signs may not occur until one or more weeks after a bite. They include any of the following: a slowly expanding red rash, fatigue, headache, flu-like symptoms, pain and stiffness in muscles and joints, fever, or swollen glands. If the disease is left untreated, arthritic-like symptoms as well as heart and nervous system complications can occur.

Note that a person may not be aware that she has been bitten by a tick. If a person suspects that she has been bitten, a doctor should be contacted as soon as possible to begin antibiotic treatment. The disease is most easily treated in its earliest stages.

First aid:

1. Remove any embedded tick with fine-pointed tweezers by grasping it very close to the skin and pulling firmly.

2. Wash the site and hands with soap and water. Apply antiseptic to the bite.

3. Save the tick on an index card or in a jar, and make a label giving the date and location of the bite.

4. Report the bite and any symptoms listed above to a doctor. Watch the area for the next month for any signs of a rash. Lyme disease is treated with antibiotics.

Storms and Natural Disasters

Be prepared for whatever natural disasters are most apt to occur in the region of the country where the trip will take place. Part of the preparation for each outdoor trip should be a review of the proper responses to the emergency situations that can result from lightning, fires, winter storms, floods, hurricanes, tornadoes, or earthquakes. Everyone should practice the procedures for seeking shelter and evacuating a site.

Lightning

In the summer, afternoon thunderstorms are common in some regions, especially at high elevations. Lightning often strikes the tallest object in the area. At the first signs of an impending storm—towering thunderheads, darkening skies, lightning and thunder, and increasing wind—seek shelter. Buildings and automobiles are safe places to seek shelter during a storm. While indoors, stay away from doors, windows, plumbing, and electrical appliances.

If caught outside during a lightning storm:

- Stay away from tall, solitary objects such as trees or electrical poles.

- Avoid standing on a hilltop, exposed ridge, or above treeline.

- If the group is in an open area, spread several yards apart.

- If swimming, get out of the water immediately and get away from the water.

- If in a small boat, return to land and seek shelter.

- Don't seek shelter in a shallow cave.

- Avoid touching things made of metal, such as a wire fence.

Human position in lighting storm.

- Move away from tent poles, aluminum canoes, and other objects that conduct electricity.

- If a sheltered area is not available, crouch low to the ground and place hands on knees or sit on a daypack or foam pad. Do not lie flat on the ground.

Give prompt first aid to anyone struck by lightning. Do not be afraid to touch or handle the victim; the victim is not electrically charged. Administer artificial respiration if the victim has stopped breathing, and treat for shock. A victim requiring cardiopulmonary resuscitation (CPR) should be treated only by a trained rescuer. Keep the victim quiet until she has been moved to a hospital. A person who appears to be unhurt or stunned should also receive first aid. Check for burns and treat for shock. Keep the victim lying down and seek medical assistance.

Fires

Everyone must be prepared for fire emergencies. Practice fire drills within 24 hours after arrival at the site. When staying in a building, make sure everyone knows how to behave during emergencies, where the exits are, and where to reassemble outside. Paths to the exits must be clear at all times. Everyone must know how to unlock the doors and windows from the inside. This allows for quick escape.

Learn how to use a fire extinguisher. Everyone should practice the proper method of extinguishing fire on clothing. Remind each girl to keep calm and roll in the dirt or on the floor (see next page). If a blanket or rug is at hand, the girl should wrap herself in the blanket and then roll on the floor or ground.

Review *Safety-Wise* and the *Junior Girl Scout Handbook* for more information on fire safety.

Stop   *Drop*   *Roll*

Teach girls what to do if clothes catch on fire. A girl should: (1) *Stop.* Do not run, walk, or jump around. (2) *Drop.* Drop to the ground and cover her face with her hands. (3) *Roll.* Smother the fire by rolling over slowly.

Wildfires. Wildfires occur most often in dry, western parts of the United States, but can occur in other areas when rainfall is low, lightning has struck the ground, or human carelessness has started a fire. When planning a hike, check on the weather and fire conditions in the area and ask authorities about any special restrictions because of the conditions. If smoke from an unknown source is seen from your campsite, check immediately with authorities and be ready to move out if told to do so.

When you are hiking keep an eye on the sky throughout the day. If you see a plume of smoke, watch to see if it gets bigger. Determine which way the wind is blowing and watch for blowing embers.

If you are in the area of a fire:

- Look for escape routes such as dirt roads, gravel areas, large outcroppings of rock, asphalt, or an already burned area. Head for one of these immediately.

- Avoid going uphill from a fire. Heat rises rapidly and the fire will outrun you up the hill.

- If smoke is a problem, cover your mouth and nose with a damp cloth. If the air becomes very hot, breathe through your nose.

- If the fire is gaining on you, look for places with the least burnable fuels. Fine grasses are a carrier of fire, so stomp and scrape an area clear with your feet if necessary.

- Stay away from trees, thickets, and brushy areas.

- Use any jacket, backpack, hat, or other items to shield yourself from heat.

- If necessary, lie down on a dirt surface with your feet pointing toward the approaching flames. (Even loose sand may give some protection if scooped over your feet or legs.)

- When the major portion of the fire has passed, continue to look for the best escape routes.

- Notify authorities when leaving the fire scene so that they know you are safe.

Winter Storms

Winter storms vary in size and strength and include blizzards, heavy snowstorms, and ice storms. When traveling or camping during the winter, take ample supplies of food, water, sleeping bags, and blankets to provide protection in case you are stranded away from shelter. Dress for cold weather in layered, loose-fitting, lightweight clothing. Know prevention and first aid procedures for hypothermia and frostbite.

If you are caught in a winter storm at an indoor camping facility:

- Listen to a local radio station to determine whether there is a storm watch or warning.

- Check battery-powered equipment, emergency cooking facilities, and other emergency gear.

- Stay inside and avoid traveling during a severe storm.

If caught outside in a winter storm:

- Try to find shelter. Pitch a tent, prepare a lean-to, seek a windbreak, or build a snow cave for protection from the wind.

- Try to stay dry and cover all exposed parts of the body.

- Build a fire for heat.

- Melt snow for drinking. Don't eat snow, as it will lower your body temperature.

- Conserve body heat and energy; do not overexert by walking in the snow.

Whether you are caught indoors or outdoors in a winter storm, use the buddy system if it is necessary to seek help.

Floods and Flash Floods

Floods can occur in almost any part of the United States and usually result from heavy or prolonged rain, rapidly melting snow, or dam breakage. Flash floods can occur with little or no warning and are dangerous because of their swift currents and unpredictable nature. The National Weather Service provides flood alerts. Radio broadcasts provide advance warnings and instructions.

Satellite photo of a hurricane over Florida.
Source: National Oceanic and Atmospheric Administration.

- When warnings are provided, evacuate the area swiftly and seek shelter. Extra food and water, flashlights, and dry clothes will be needed.

- Never camp in dry river beds in areas where an upstream thunderstorm could produce a flash flood.

- If evacuation is not possible, determine the best route to high ground. Individuals should not attempt to wade through water higher than knee-deep. Once high ground is reached, wait for rescue parties.

Hurricanes

The following safety rules should be considered before, during, and after a hurricane:

- Listen for warnings on the radio. Have a battery-operated radio available in case of power failure.

- Stay away from beaches or other locations that may be swept by tides or storm waves.

- Watch for high water in areas where streams or rivers may flood after heavy rain.

- If in a camp building, board up all windows.

- Store extra food and water.

- Make sure vehicles have gas.

- Seek shelter indoors, away from windows.

- Use the telephone only for emergencies.

- Leave sites that might be affected by storm, tide, stream flooding, or falling trees.

- Drive or walk to the nearest designated shelter, using recommended evacuation routes.

- Do not be fooled by the "eye" of the storm (calm period). Winds from the other direction will soon pick up.

- After the storm, stay away from disaster areas. Watch for dangling electrical wires, roads undermined by rushing water, flooded low spots, or fires. Drive cautiously.

Tornadoes

A tornado is often considered nature's most violent storm because of its destructive force. Tornadoes occur more often in the spring in the central United States than anywhere else on earth. Darkened skies, thick storm clouds, and strong winds from the south, combined with lightning and periods of rain and hail, often precede a tornado's arrival.

If a tornado warning is issued, take a battery-powered radio and head for a protected area immediately.

Safe places to take shelter include:

- Storm shelters and basements
- Caves
- Tunnels and underground parking facilities
- Interior corridors or hallways
- Steel-framed or reinforced buildings

Dangerous places that should be avoided include:

- Cars, house trailers, and parked vehicles
- Tents
- Structures with large, poorly supported roofs
- Gymnasiums or auditoriums
- Indoors near windows, doors, and outside walls

If caught outside, don't try to outrun the tornado. Move away by taking a route that is at right angles to the tornado's path. If there is no time to escape, lie flat in a ditch, ravine, culvert, or under a bridge and protect your head.

Earthquakes

Earthquakes occur most frequently along fault lines west of the Rocky Mountains, but there is the potential for them in most states. The greatest danger in an earth-

quake is the falling debris. Keep the following safety rules in mind when faced with an earthquake:

- Keep calm. Don't panic or run.
- If outdoors, get away from buildings, walls, utility poles, or power lines. Head for clear areas.
- If indoors, stand in a doorway or lie under a heavy piece of furniture such as a desk, table, or bed. Stay away from windows.
- After an earthquake, be careful when entering a damaged building.
- Don't touch downed power lines or any objects in contact with them.
- Listen to a portable radio to get the latest emergency information. Be prepared for aftershocks.
- Cooperate with public safety officials.

Dealing with Medical Emergencies and Personal Issues

Many activities in Girl Scouting are carried out close to home, within reach of family and community support services. In a crisis, medical attention or counseling services can usually be obtained fairly quickly. If there is a medical emergency or a fire, girls need to be taught to call the emergency rescue number in their community. Traveling troops staying at camps, hotels, or at Girl Scout troop houses have access to professional services offered in the community being visited.

If a girl becomes ill or is injured, after appropriate first aid is administered, assess the situation to see if she can continue on the trip. If the itinerary permits and the illness or injury is not too serious, the group may elect to stay at the campsite an extra day or two to give the girl time to recover. If the situation is more serious and she cannot be moved, help may need to be summoned while the girl is given appropriate care and made comfortable.

If the girl can travel, several options are available. If she needs medical attention, an adult should accompany her to a place where she can get the help she needs while the rest of the group continues with the trip. This option is possible only if there is sufficient adult coverage to divide the group. In some cases, the trip may need to be terminated and the resources of the entire group utilized to get the girl to safety. Or, the leaders may determine that the trip will finish early because proper adult coverage is no longer possible.

On a wilderness adventure away from conventional assistance, leaders and girls need to plan ahead and be more resourceful if an emergency or problem occurs. Camping together often promotes an atmosphere of openness and honesty where girls feel free to share and to discuss things that are happening to them at school or at home. A girl may choose to talk with her peers or confide in her leader about concerns that have not previously been disclosed. Problems may include dealing with illness or injury, threatened or attempted suicide, substance abuse, emotional disorders, or distress related to an event in a girl's life such as divorce of parents or death of a family member.

See *Safety-Wise* (pages 25–28) for general tips on how to handle these sensitive issues, as well as the physical and behavioral symptoms of these problems. Take time to review these tips and help the girl to find appropriate help.

Seeking assistance. Know and follow your local council's procedures about immediate notification of council staff if a serious situation arises. The council staff has developed contacts within the council jurisdiction and in communities close to Girl Scout facilities to deal with emergencies. These procedures should be available before the trip as well as at sites operated by the Girl Scout council. Common sense and flexibility are important factors to consider when it becomes necessary to seek assistance for an injured or seriously distressed girl.

Chapter 6

Compass and Map Skills

Our earliest ancestors navigated by the sun, stars, currents, and prevailing winds. They used rough sketch maps and route descriptions from other travelers to find their way. Explorers marked trails by etching blaze marks on trees and laid trail signs. With the invention of the compass, people learned to navigate from point to point with reliability and confidence.

As girls become progressively more skillful, they may wish to venture beyond the troop meeting place or established campsite to explore new places. Help girls learn to use a map and compass and introduce them to orienteering. These skills are fun and will provide each girl with the navigational tools necessary for many outdoor activities.

Finding Directions Using the Sun and Stars

The sun can indicate general directions. In the morning, the sun rises in the east. To locate approximate north, turn the right shoulder toward the early morning sun and you are facing north. In the late afternoon, the sun is in the western sky. To locate approximate north, turn the left shoulder toward the sun. You are now facing north.

N ←

Determining north by turning the right shoulder to the sun in the morning.

On a sunny day, an analog wristwatch can be used to find north (see above). Hold the watch level in the sun. Hold a tiny stick vertically over the center point of the watch so a shadow falls on the watch face. Rotate the watch until the shadow lies over the hour hand. In the afternoon, north is the point halfway between the hour hand and the number 12 going the shortest way around the face of the watch.

On a clear night, the North Star (Polaris) will indicate the location of north. Since the North Star is not a particularly bright star, use the two stars that form the outside of the bowl of the Big Dipper to locate the North Star (see next page). Estimate approximately seven times the distance between these two stars to determine the distance from the Big Dipper to the North Star. By facing the North Star, you will be looking north. Once the North Star has been located, other directions can be found.

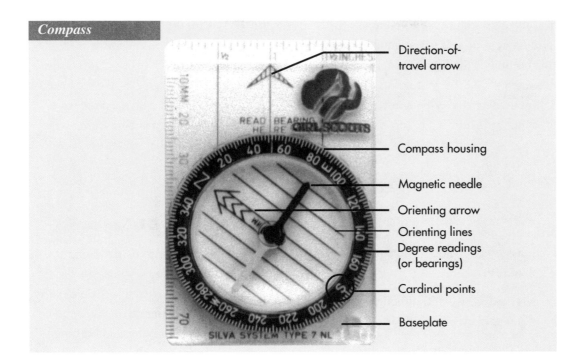

Direction-of-travel arrow

Compass housing

Magnetic needle

Orienting arrow

Orienting lines

Degree readings (or bearings)

Cardinal points

Baseplate

Compass Use

A compass determines direction through use of a steel needle attracted by the magnetism of the earth. When at rest, the compass needle points to the north end of this giant magnet. Magnetic north is different from the geographic or map-north indicated on most maps.

To orient a compass to north, hold it level in front of the body and turn the compass housing until the N on the compass lines up with the red tip of the compass needle. When north is located, east (E), west (W), south (S), and all the points in between can then be located. When using a compass, be careful not to hold it close to anything that might have magnetic properties or the needle will point toward the object and not toward north (N).

The numbers on a compass are called degrees or bearings. A compass has 360 degrees, indicated by the symbol °. The reading 90° is the same as east.

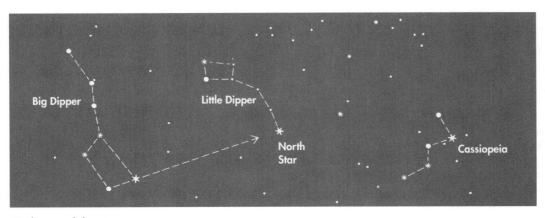

Finding north by stars.

The most efficient type of compass for land navigation is a baseplate compass that combines the features of a compass dial with those of a protractor. The following terms may be helpful when teaching girls to use a baseplate compass:

Direction-of-travel arrow—points in the direction to go after the compass bearing is set.

Magnetic needle—moves inside the compass housing and always points north when at rest.

Degree readings—360 directions that can be traveled from any point.

Baseplate—shows direction-of-travel arrow and a scale of millimeters and inches for computing distance on a map.

Compass housing—"houses" the needle.

Orienting arrow—stationary arrow inside the housing.

Orienting lines—parallel lines inside the compass housing.

Using the Compass to Follow Direction

To travel 270° or head west, turn the compass housing until 270° is in line with the direction-of-travel arrow. Hold the compass level in the hand with the direction-of-travel arrow pointing straight ahead. Orient the compass by moving your entire body until the orienting arrow is right underneath the magnetic needle and pointing in the same direction. The compass bearer is now facing 270°. Site a landmark in the distance in line with the direction of the travel arrow. You will be walking west as you walk toward that landmark.

Determining Distance

One of the first steps in using a map is to learn how distance represented on a map compares to the distance to be traveled by foot. One way to estimate distance is to count steps while walking and multiply the number of steps by the length of one's steps. The easiest way to do this is to figure the length of one's pace (the distance covered in two steps). Here's how to determine the length of a pace:

1. Mark off a pace course by putting a marker at each end of the measured distance. For this example, 30 meters and 100 feet are used. Determine the pace in both feet and meters because USGS (U.S. Geographical Survey) topographical maps are drawn in feet and orienteering maps are drawn in meters.

2. Have the girl walk from one end of the course to the other in her normal stride. She should count the number of paces taken. (Have her count each time she puts down her right foot or left, whichever is preferred.)

3. Repeat two more times.

4. Add together the number of paces taken each time and divide by three to get the average number of paces taken in the measured distance.

Metric	U.S. Equivalent
on a 30-meter pace course:	on a 100-foot pace course:
20 paces (first time)	21 paces (first time)
22 paces (second time)	19 paces (second time)
+ 18 paces (third time)	+ 20 paces (third time)
60 paces	60 paces
60 ÷ 3 = 20 (average number of paces)	60 ÷ 3 = 20 (average number of paces)

5. To find the length of the girl's average pace, divide the distance by the average number of paces.

$$\frac{\text{Distance}}{\text{Average number of paces}} = \text{Length of average pace}$$

In this example:

Metric	U.S. Equivalent
$\dfrac{30 \text{ meters}}{20 \text{ paces}} = 1.5$ meters per pace	$\dfrac{100 \text{ feet}}{20 \text{ paces}} = 5$ feet per pace

It is important to remember the length of the pace. Now a girl can estimate distance whenever she wishes. Simply count the number of paces it takes to cover an unknown distance and multiply this by the length of the pace.

For example:

Metric	U.S. Equivalent
93 paces x 1.5 meters per pace =	75 paces x 5 feet per pace =
139.5 meters traveled	375 feet traveled

A person's pace will differ if she is running or on hilly or rough terrain. Girls may wish to measure their pace in a variety of walking and running conditions so that their estimates of distance will be as accurate as possible.

Elements of a Topographical Map

Name

GARFIELD QUADRANGLE
NEW MEXICO
7.5 MINUTE SERIES (TOPOGRAPHIC)

Preparation Date

Mapped, edited, and published by the Geological Survey

Control by USGS and NOS/NOAA

Topography by photogrammetric methods from aerial photographs taken 1958. Field checked 1961

Inset Showing Location

NEW MEXICO

QUADRANGLE LOCATION

Scale

Distance Rulers

SCALE 1:24 000

1000   0   1000   2000   3000   4000   5000   6000   7000 FEET

1   .5   0   1 KILOMETER

1 MILE

Contour Intervals

CONTOUR INTERVAL 20 FEET

Map Symbols

Highway (red)	Power transmission line
Light duty road	Telephone line
Unimproved road	Topographic contours (brown)
Trail	Depression (brown)
Bridge (red)	Hill (brown)
Dwelling	Quarry
School, church	Sand or mud area (brown)
Barn, warehouse	Woods (green)
Airport	Orchard (green)
Water tank	Stream (blue)
Campground, picnic area	River (blue)
Cemetery	Marsh or swamp (blue)
Railroad	Water well; spring (blue)

Map Colors

Black: Cultural features such as roads and buildings
Blue: Water features such as lakes and rivers
Brown: Features showing elevation changes
Green: Woodland cover
Red: Important roads
Purple: Features added from aerial photographs

Declination

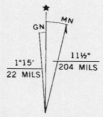

GN   MN

1°15'
22 MILS

11½°
204 MILS

UTM GRID AND 1980 MAGNETIC NORTH
DECLINATION AT CENTER OF SHEET

Reading and Using Maps

A map is a two-dimensional drawing that represents an area of the earth's surface. There are many types of maps, including rough sketch, highway, topographical, orienteering, and engineering. Become familiar with maps by studying a local road or topographical map. A topographical map provides additional information about the contours and surface features of an area. Most topographical maps are drawn by the U.S. Geological Survey/Department of the Interior. These maps include the following vital information:

· **Preparation date:** The date it was prepared, last checked in the field, and redrawn.

· **Inset showing location:** An inset drawing of the state with a square designating the location of the map.

· **Scale:** A scale; USGS topographical maps are often drawn 1:24,000. This means that one inch on the map represents 24,000 inches, or 2,000 feet, on the ground.

· **Distance rulers:** Rulers with bars divided into miles, feet, and kilometers.

· **Contour intervals:** These lines show the distance between two adjacent contour lines. They help to determine whether the terrain is flat or steep.

· **Map symbols.**

· **Map colors:** Colors that symbolize certain features, such as blue for water, brown for land.

· **Declination:** The angle between the direction the compass needle points (magnetic north) and the geographic or true North Pole of the Earth.

· **North/south or meridian lines.** These lines indicate true north.

Orient a map by turning it until the north side of the map is aligned in the same direction as the magnetic needle of the compass. Explore the map, sighting landmarks with a compass along the way. If the group traveled east 120°, what would they see? Practice map reading by making up questions that can be answered by using the map.

Declination

Since the compass needle points to magnetic north rather than true north, it is important to ascertain the local declination. An orienteering map drawn to the area's declination may be available. If not, corrections for declination must be made or the route will be incorrect.

Let's say the degree of declination is 5°W and the compass reading for the destination is 282°. Add 5° to 282° and get 287°. Reset the direction-of-travel arrow at 287° by turning the compass housing and proceed.

If the declination is east, subtract the degree of declination from the compass reading for the destination. For example, if the degree of declination is 10° E and the compass reading for the destination is 144°, reset the compass to 134° (10° subtracted from 144°).

An easy way to remember this information is to memorize this rhyme:

Declination West—Compass Best (add degrees of declination)

Declination East—Compass Least (subtract degrees of declination)

Drawing a Sketch Map

If a map of an area does not exist or if the scale is too small, draw a sketch map. Follow these steps:

1. Select the area for mapping. Establish a starting point at or near a clearly recognizable feature.

2. Take field notes describing the direction, distance, and features for each leg of your path. Note the degree reading on the compass for each direction of travel. Count the number of paces between landmarks. Document this information in an orderly way.

3. Before drawing the map, change paces into distance traveled. (Multiply the number of paces counted by the length of your pace and select a map scale that allows large distances to fit the size of paper being used.)

4. Develop a scale for the map. For example:

Metric
If 600 meters of landscape must fit on a piece of paper 30 centimeters wide, each centimeter on the map could represent 20 meters of distance traveled. Scale: 1 centimeter = 20 meters.

U.S. Equivalent
If 100 feet of landscape must fit on a 12-inch piece of paper, one inch on the map could represent ten feet of the distance traveled. Scale: 1 inch = 10 feet.

5. Change all the distances traveled in the field to map measurements.

6. Draw the map. First, be sure that there are no metal objects nearby or metal parts to the worktable. On a large sheet of paper, label the top edge "North" and draw a north directional arrow in the corner. Draw parallel guidelines to represent N-S lines. Turn the paper around slowly, with the compass on it, until the magnetic needle aligns with the arrow in the corner of the map. Do not move the paper from this position during the following steps. (Tape down the corners.)

Turn the compass housing to line up the direction-of-travel arrow with the first degree reading from the field notes. In the example on the next page, the compass was set at 18°.

Place the compass on the paper with the orienting arrow parallel to the N-S lines and pointing toward the map's north.

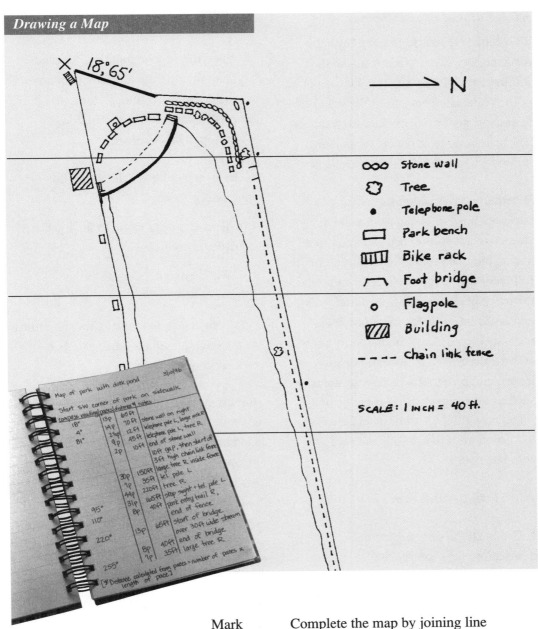

Mark an "X" on the paper to indicate the starting point. Draw a line along the long side of the compass base. This line represents the direction traveled during the first leg of the path.

Make the line equal in length to the scale distance for the first segment of the path.

Add landmarks to the map at the correct places, as noted in the field notes.

Complete the map by joining line segments that represent sections of the path traveled.

To create a map legend, note the scale used and identify the symbols. Add the names of the mapmakers, the date made, and the location of the map. Names of places can be added where appropriate to help a map user locate the setting and features of the map.

Hiking with Map and Compass

To calculate distance, first measure the distance between two points using the millimeter (or inch) ruler on the base plate of the compass. Then check the map scale to convert map measurement to distance. This can be done in meters or feet, or in kilometers or miles for longer distances.

Whether in preparation for a hike or a backpacking trip, the map should be studied in advance to select a main route and an alternate route. Trails should be followed whenever possible to minimize the trampling of fragile vegetation and erodable soils. If off-trail travel is necessary, consider obstacles such as cliffs and stream crossings, elevation gains and losses, and potentially hazardous areas such as a swamp or the knife edge of a ridge. As a rule, off-trail travel between two locations will not follow a straight compass course.

When hiking with a map and compass:

1. Establish the direction of the destination, for example, 95°.

2. Set the compass and remember to correct for declination.

3. Face the direction of travel. Sight a landmark in the distance (tree, large rock, etc.).

4. Walk to the landmark.

5. When the first landmark is reached, sight along the direction-of-travel arrow on the compass to find another landmark along the route to the destination. Continue in this manner.

6. To go around obstacles (with no landmarks ahead):

(a) Turn at a right angle to the intended course and count paces.

(b) Walk a parallel course to the intended route.

(c) Turn at a right angle again and return to the course with the same number of paces counted.

Backsighting. To determine that a person is on the right course, "backsight" the last landmark. With the direction-of-travel arrow still set for the intended course, turn the body around until the *south end* of the magnetic needle settles over the north end of the orienting arrow. If the direction-of-travel arrow now points toward the last landmark, the person is on course.

Aiming off. When heading toward an exact location such as the junction of two trails, it is a good practice to deliberately aim slightly either to the left or right of the junction. When a girl intersects with a trail, she will know which way to turn to find the junction.

50°
Forward
course

Last
landmark

Backsighting.

Aiming off.

Steps in using a map and compass

1. Place the long edge of the compass along the route from the starting point to the destination.

2. Turn the compass housing until the orienting lines in the base of the compass are parallel to the vertical (north-south) lines on the map.

3. Lift the compass from the map. Place the compass flat on the hand with the direction-of-travel arrow pointing away from the body. Move the feet until the magnetic needle aligns with the orienting arrow. Sight along the direction-of-travel arrow to a landmark in the distance.

6

Orienteering

Another way to utilize map and compass skills is to take part in orienteering as a competitive sport or recreational activity. Orienteering is navigating through unfamiliar terrain to find a series of natural or built features with the aid of a map and compass. Orienteering is generally done in a forested area but may be carried out on any site that has been mapped, even a shopping mall.

Orienteering Maps

An orienteering map is a very detailed topographical map. It shows all the significant natural features such as cliffs, boulders, wetlands, vegetation, and built features such as buildings, fences, and power lines. The scale of an orienteering map is often 1:15,000. (The scale of USGS topographical maps is usually too large to be used for orienteering.) Orienteering maps are painstakingly prepared by field checkers who map the details of the terrain and cartographers who prepare the finished product.

Orienteering maps around the world use identical symbols and colors. The symbols and their interpretations are printed in the legend.

The legend of an orienteering map uses symbols similar to those on a topographical map but also indicates which areas are crossable or difficult to navigate on foot.

Examples:

Fence

Uncrossable fence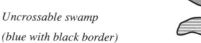

Lake (blue with black border)

Uncrossable swamp (blue with black border)

Thick vegetation (green)

Orienteering maps also show small details like boulders, rock outcroppings, and fences that would not appear on other maps. These help to pinpoint the location of control points.

The major colors are:

- Brown—contour features that show the shape of the land and changes in elevation

- Blue—water features such as streams, swamps, and lakes

- Green—thick vegetation

- Orange—open fields and semi-open areas

- Black—built features such as buildings, roads, and trails as well as rock features such as cliffs and boulders

- White—open wooded areas

It is good practice to look at the legend to see if some of the features shown on the map itself are easily recognizable. Have the girls try picturing what an area might look like; then later have them go there and see how close they were.

With an orienteering map, a girl does not have to adjust her compass for the declination of the area. The north-south lines are drawn indicating magnetic north.

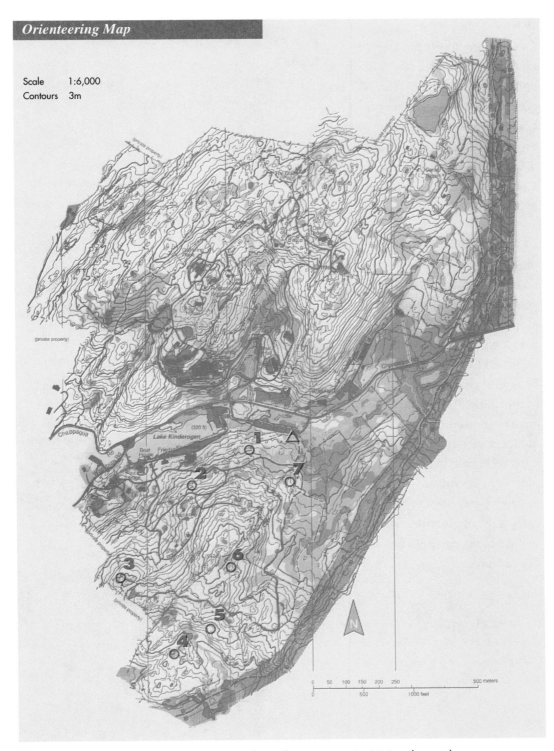

Orienteering Map

Scale   1:6,000
Contours   3m

The southern section of this orienteering map shows the starting point (△) and control points (○) for an orienteering course. Each point is visited in the numbered order. Decide how to get from point to point by using map reading skills and compass readings.

Orienteering Meets

Orienteering meets are sponsored by local clubs. At a meet, a number of different courses are usually offered. A course consists of a series of locations called control points that the navigator must visit. Each course is designed to test different levels of ability to navigate. Courses are designed to take into account age, sex, physical fitness, and experience.

At the beginning of the meet, participants may be given maps with a pre-drawn course or they may have to copy the course from a master map. The starting point is shown on the map by a triangle. Each control point to be visited is indicated by a circle on the map. The feature to be located is in the exact center of the circle. Each control point has a control code consisting of letters or numbers in parentheses. Control points must be visited in numerical order unless otherwise instructed. As a further aid in locating the control points, navigators carry a list of clues describing the feature found in the center of each of the circles. For example:

	Control Code	Clue
Control Point 1:	(BZ)	Junction of trail and stream
Control Point 2:	(TL)	Boulder—1 meter—north side
Control Point 3:	(43)	Building—south side

At each control point there will be an orange and white marker with the control code attached. To prove that the navigator has reached the correct marker, she will punch her score card.

Orienteering is a thinking person's activity. Often the person who selects the best route will finish faster than a quick runner. As with any other activity, some basic safety precautions are necessary:

- Always carry a compass and know how to use it.

- Know the safety bearing—a degree reading for the orienteering course that will bring the participant back to a major road or other recognizable feature.

- Be sure to check in at the finish line of the course.

Orienteering control marker.

Brownie Girl Scouts finding their way along a string-O course.

String Orienteering

String orienteering, also known as string-O, is a way to introduce Daisy and Brownie Girl Scouts to orienteering. A large-scale map is drawn. A colorful string is laid along the course, which has 10 to 12 control points fairly close together. Each control point is shown on the map. Using maps, the girls follow the string, which is indicated as a line on the map. As they reach each control point, the girls mark their score cards with crayons or place stickers at each number. The string eventually leads the girls to the finish area.

To design a string course, be creative and try to select features that would interest a girl, such as a large tree or boulder. Be sure to select a site for the string course away from poison ivy, road crossings, or any other hazards.

Once young girls understand that a map represents the features they see around them, they can begin to read different kinds of maps and find locations on them. They can practice by using a map of an indoor space like a classroom or meeting room to find specially placed markers in the room.

Outside, they can use a map of the school grounds or local park to go on a treasure hunt or find answers to questions like: "What shape are the leaves on the tree at this location?" Girls can also draw their own maps of a playground, their neighborhood, or other favorite places. (See examples on pages 18 and 34.)

Map reading skills are a primary component of orienteering. They give girls the knowledge and confidence to explore new places. The sport of orienteering is fun for all age levels, teaches decision-making skills, and leads to self-confidence and a sense of achievement.

To learn more about orienteering, contact the United States Orienteering Federation, P.O. Box 1444, Forest Park, Georgia 30051, for a list of clubs by state.

Chapter 7

Understanding Our Environment

Being outdoors gives girls opportunities to see and experience firsthand seasonal changes, weather phenomena, and other parts of our environment we often know little about. Understanding the basics about seasons, weather, and geology can help to make time in the outdoors safer and increase understanding of how our activities can alter the environment if we are not careful.

What Makes Seasons?

Girls can enhance their understanding of our Earth and its seasons by enacting what happens to the Earth, sun, and moon during a year's time. Girls can form a large oval outdoors or in a large indoor space. Use a compass to determine which direction is north. Post a sign for north or ask one girl to hold the sign. Provide three balls or balloons of different sizes. A large yellow beach ball, balloon, or a basketball could represent the sun. One girl sits in the middle of the oval holding the "sun." Another girl holds a smaller ball or balloon representing the Earth. A blue one would be a good representation of our "ocean planet" as it appears from outer space. A third girl holds a small ball, such as a table tennis ball, to represent the moon.

1. Start by asking the girls to describe how the Earth and the sun move around each other. When the girl holding the "Earth" walks around the oval formed by the group in a counterclockwise direction, she is following a path similar to the Earth's revolution around the sun. How long does this take? (365 days.) Practice this movement once.

2. The Earth's seasons occur because the Earth spins around an axis that is tilted toward a particular position in the universe. We call this direction north. The girl who is holding the "Earth" should show how the Earth spins on its axis and try to walk around the oval at the same time. Make sure she is spinning the Earth in the correct direction. That is what makes our weather fronts travel from west to east across the country as the Earth's rotation pulls the atmosphere with it.

3. Now the "moon" can be added. Talk about the path of the moon around the Earth and how long that takes. (About 27 days.) Ask the girls representing the moon and the Earth to demonstrate how the moon moves around the Earth. (The moon travels in a counterclockwise direction around the Earth, and the same side of the moon always faces the Earth.)

4. Now try putting it all together! The Earth moves on its oval path around the sun while spinning and keeping the North Pole pointed toward north. The moon travels around the Earth about 13 times in its yearly journey. Try this demonstration one more time, stopping in each of the four seasons to show the relationship between the Earth and the sun and talk about where the northern hemisphere is in relationship to the sun. (Girls in the oval could even be lined up by their birthdays so that they can see the relationship as the year progresses.)

Girl on the left holds a large ball to represent the sun. Girl in the center shows the movement of the Earth around the sun.

The tilt of the axis of the Earth as it spins creates our seasonal variations in temperatures.

The girl on the left holding the moon shows the counter-clockwise path of the moon around the Earth.

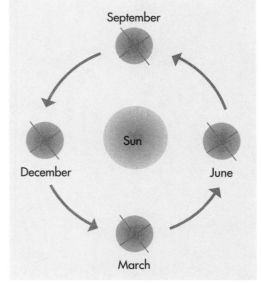

The Earth moves in an elliptical path around the sun once a year. Have girls with balls stop in each of the four positions represented here to see how the position of the Earth changes in relation to the sun with the seasons.

Weather

Predicting the weather is an important skill for many outdoor activities. Changing weather conditions may force a change in plans in order to avoid stormy conditions, or may provide an unexpected opportunity to enjoy an outdoor activity.

Weather is the condition of the atmosphere at any given time or place, and includes air pressure, moisture, wind, and temperature. Tracking the indicators of weather can be fun and can help develop an understanding of weather patterns.

Air Masses

Changes in weather are primarily due to movement of air masses with different temperatures and moisture content. The movement of these air masses is caused by many factors including the Earth's rotation, unequal heating of the Earth at the poles and equator, and irregular surface features of the Earth. Air masses that sit over oceans or land masses take on various characteristics of temperature and moisture that they carry with them as they move into new areas.

When air masses with different characteristics come in contact with each other, clouds form and precipitation often results.

Warm and cold fronts create predictable patterns of clouds, as shown on the next page.

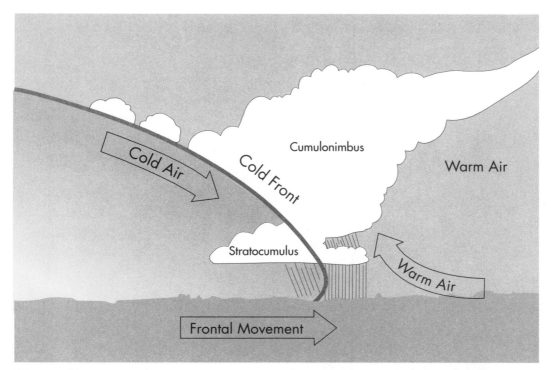

When a cold air mass pushes into a warmer air mass, the warmer air is pushed upward. As the warm air is pushed up, it cools and the moisture in it condenses into clouds. With enough moisture, rain or snow may be formed. Rapidly moving cold fronts can also cause thunderstorms and tornadoes.

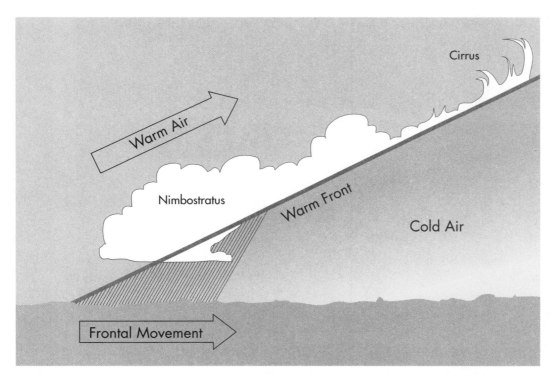

At other times, a warm air mass may replace a cold one. The warm air rides up over the colder air. Where the two air masses contact each other, clouds are formed and rain or snow can result.

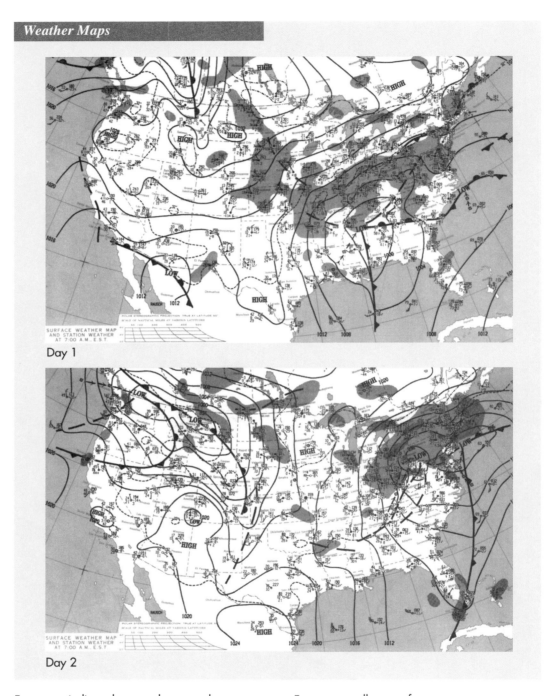

Day 1

Day 2

Fronts are indicated on weather maps by bold lines.

Warm front moving east

Cold front moving south

Stationary front

Fronts generally move from west to east across the United States. Note how the low pressure in the Southeast moved to the Northeast, carrying precipitation with it. New low-pressure systems were generated in the Pacific during this period and then traveled across the country.

Use weather maps from several successive days to predict what your local weather will be.

Activity Suggestion

Reading Weather Maps

Compare weather maps for several days in a row to see how weather fronts move across the United States and affect your part of the country. These patterns vary with the seasons.

Clouds

Clouds are made of water vapor or ice crystals. There are three distinct types of clouds; each has a different appearance and is easily recognized. Cirrus clouds are high, thin, and wispy. Cumulus clouds are billowy and dome-shaped (like mounds of cotton). Stratus clouds are low, flat, and layered. The word "nimbus" combined with one of these terms indicates precipitation.

Watch the cloud patterns over a period of 12 to 24 hours to predict the weather.

Cirrus clouds

Cumulus clouds

Stratus clouds

Barometric Pressure

Another way to measure an air mass is to measure its weight. Cold air weighs more than warm air because its molecules are closer together. A barometer allows us to measure the weight of the air mass above us. By watching whether the air pressure is rising or falling on a barometer, we can determine whether a high- or low-pressure system is approaching. Each of these systems has different characteristics, as shown on the next page.

Air Temperature

Air temperatures are due primarily to the sun's energy. Many factors can cause temperatures to fluctuate. The longer the sun shines and the more direct the angle of the rays, the greater the warming effect.

Activity Suggestion

Using a Thermometer

Take air temperature each day at approximately the same time in the same place, using a thermometer held at chest height and not directly in the sun. A local hardware store is a good source for thermometers. Try taking the temperature in a variety of locations; have girls find warm and cool spots.

Barometer.

Also, try taking five air temperature readings in a day:

1. Just before sunrise (usually the coldest)

2. Midmorning

3. Midafternoon

4. Just before nightfall

5. Before bedtime

What patterns have the girls found?

High-Pressure System

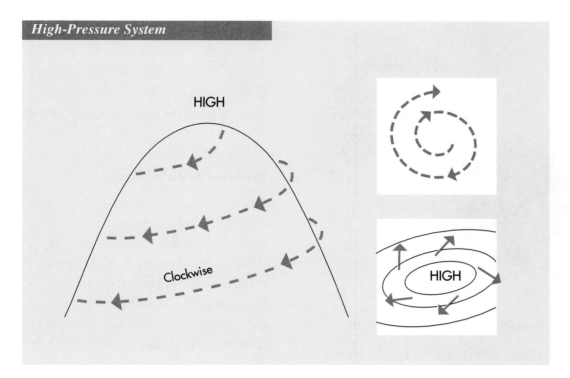

The air in a high-pressure system moves in a large, clockwise spiral and usually brings clear and fair weather.

Low-Pressure System

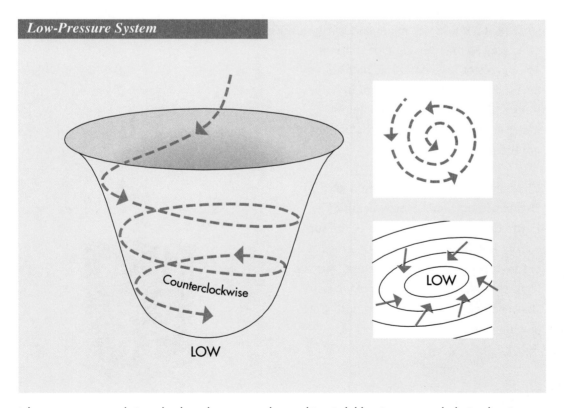

A low-pressure system brings cloudy and stormy weather, and its winds blow in a counterclockwise direction.

Activity Suggestion

Sunshine Warms the Earth

The effect of the sun's rays in heating the Earth can be seen by filling two trays with soil to a depth of 1 to 2 inches. Prop one tray so that the sun's rays strike the surface at a 90-degree angle and lay the other tray so that the angle of sunlight is 45 degrees or less. After one half hour, take the temperature of the soil in both trays and compare. (Push the thermometer gently into the soil so that it does not break.)

Changes in air temperature are due to changes in the sun's energy heating the Earth. On a cloudy day, some of the sun's energy is reflected back into outer space before it can warm the atmosphere. Surface features—such as large bodies of water, slope, and plant or snow cover—also affect how much the air heats.

Precipitation

Precipitation is any moisture that falls from the sky. The temperature of the air near the ground determines the form of precipitation—for example, rain, snow, sleet, or hail.

Activity Suggestion

Making a Rain Gauge

To make a gauge to measure rainfall, place a straight-sided cylindrical container in an open area to collect rain. Be careful to avoid places where the container may collect runoff from trees, buildings, or tents. Measure rainfall by holding a ruler alongside the column of water. Record the amount in the weather observations chart (see page 131) and then empty the container so that it is ready for the next reading.

Humidity

Humidity is the amount of water vapor mixed in the air. The higher the humidity, the more slowly water evaporates; the lower the humidity, the more quickly water evaporates. Evaporation occurring from our skin helps to lower the body temperature and is critical to keeping our bodies cool when the temperatures are warm.

Activity Suggestion

Making a Psychrometer

A psychrometer, which measures humidity, can be made from two thermometers. To make a psychrometer, take the two thermometers and slip a

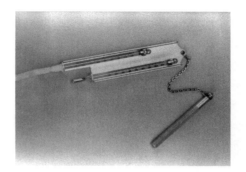

Psychrometer.

piece of white shoelace or cloth over the bulb of one thermometer. Wet the cloth with water. Take air temperature readings with the second thermometer. To determine the humidity, take a reading from each thermometer and compare the results using the chart below.

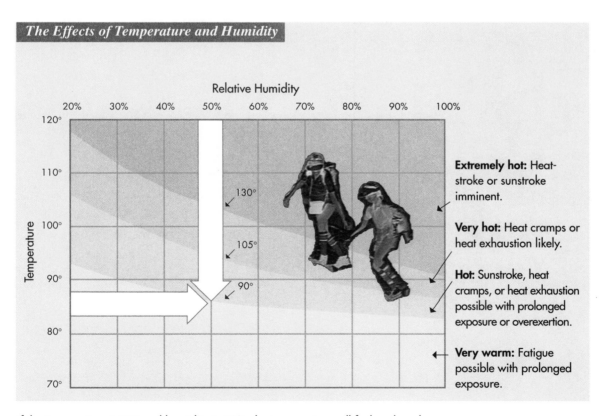

The Effects of Temperature and Humidity

Relative Humidity

Extremely hot: Heat-stroke or sunstroke imminent.

Very hot: Heat cramps or heat exhaustion likely.

Hot: Sunstroke, heat cramps, or heat exhaustion possible with prolonged exposure or overexertion.

Very warm: Fatigue possible with prolonged exposure.

If the temperature is 85° and humidity is 50%, the temperature will feel as though it is 90°.

Source: American Red Cross.

Wind

Wind is the movement of air and is caused primarily by the unequal heating of the Earth's surface. Air moves from areas of high pressure to those of low pressure. The direction of air movement is also caused by the rotation of the Earth.

Wind direction and speed are both important to consider when charting weather conditions. Wind speed is usually measured using an instrument called an anemometer. Girls can find directions for making one in a weather book from the library or from a science teacher. Visual clues in the environment can also be used and compared to the Beaufort Scale to determine wind speed (see next page).

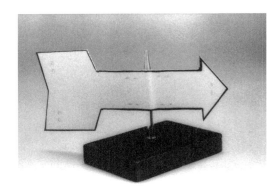

Anemometer.

Activity Suggestion

Constructing a Wind Vane

Mount a directional arrow (with the tail of the arrow broader than the head) on top of a stand that will allow the arrow to pivot freely. Determine north-south-east-west directions with a compass. The directional arrow of the wind vane will point in the direction the wind is coming from. Wind direction is always described by the direction the wind is coming from.

The wind can have a significant impact on how weather conditions affect us. Cooling winds off the ocean can make a hot summer day bearable. However, when wind is added to low temperatures, the results can be deadly if we are not prepared with appropriate clothing or shelter.

Beaufort Scale of Wind Velocity

Land Indicators	U.S. Weather Bureau Terms	Approximate Wind Speed (Miles per Hour)
Air is calm; smoke rises vertically	Calm	Less than 1
Wind causes smoke to drift, but does not move weather vanes	Light air	1–3
Wind is felt on face; leaves rustle; wind moves simple weather vanes	Light breeze	4–7
Leaves and small twigs are in constant motion; wind extends light flag	Gentle breeze	8–12
Wind raises dust and loose paper; small branches move	Moderate breeze	13–18
Small trees with full leaves sway; crested wavelets form on inland waters	Fresh breeze	19–24
Large branches are in motion; using umbrellas causes difficulty	Strong breeze	25–31
Whole trees move; walking against wind causes some difficulty	Moderate gale	32–38
Wind breaks twigs off trees and generally impedes progress when walking	Fresh gale	39–46
Wind causes slight structural damage (for instance, chimney pots and slate removed)	Strong gale	47–54
Trees are uprooted; considerable structural damage occurs (seldom experienced inland)	Whole gale	55–63
Widespread damage (very rarely experienced on land)	Storm	64–72
Violence and destruction (very rarely experienced)	Hurricane force	73 or higher

The Effects of Wind Chill

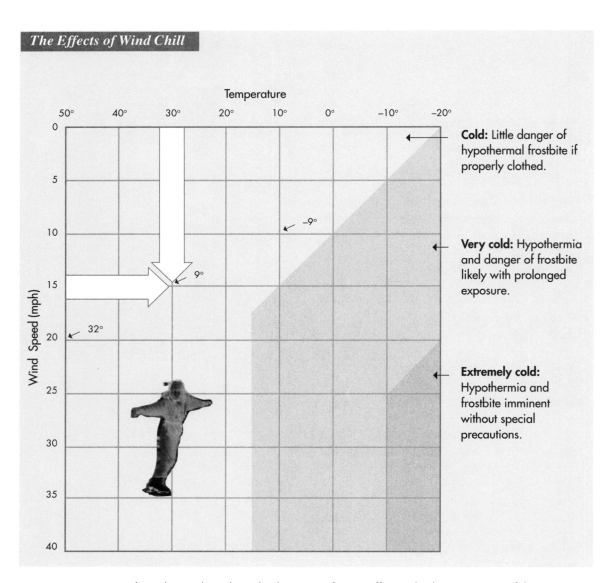

Temperature

| 50° | 40° | 30° | 20° | 10° | 0° | –10° | –20° |

Wind Speed (mph): 0, 5, 10, 15, 20, 25, 30, 35, 40

–9°

9°

32°

Cold: Little danger of hypothermal frostbite if properly clothed.

Very cold: Hypothermia and danger of frostbite likely with prolonged exposure.

Extremely cold: Hypothermia and frostbite imminent without special precautions.

Temperature, humidity, and wind are the three main factors affecting body temperature. If the temperature is 30° and the wind speed is 15 m.p.h., the temperature will feel as though it is 9°.

Source: American Red Cross.

Weather Prediction

Use a chart like the one below to record weather information and predictions for the future. Use changes in barometric pressure and clouds to predict the weather conditions for the next day.

By taking readings from places all over the world and using satellite images, meteorologists are able to create weather maps—that is, pictorial representations of weather conditions (see examples on page 122). By looking at a series of maps, they can see how fast and in what direction the air masses are moving and predict what conditions will arrive in a particular location. Using this technology, meteorologists can provide predictions for a few days into the future, and make more general forecasts for the weeks ahead.

Activity Suggestion

Learning about Meteorology

Visit a local weather station or meet with personnel at a television station to find out about the techniques they have for predicting the weather.

	Date: Time:	Date: Time:	Date: Time:
Observations			
Air temperature			
Wind direction			
Wind speed			
Cloud conditions			
Humidity			
Barometric pressure			
Precipitation			
Prediction for next 12 hours			

Soil

Soil is composed of rock particles, plant and animal matter, air, and water. Soils of different types are a result of the local climate, vegetation, and rock from which the soil was formed. There are more than 70,000 types of soil in the United States. The rock particles are the result of many different processes, including the following:

- Particles eroding from rock surfaces when they are exposed to wind, water, and temperature changes.

- Water caught in crevices freezing and expanding and causing rocks to break apart.

- Rocks moving along stream bottoms and depositing smaller rock particles.

- Roots of plants secreting acids that break down rocks.

- Glacial movement rubbing rock surfaces together to create particles.

In each case, rocks are reduced to smaller particles that become mixed with organic materials (decomposing plants and animals). The formation of soil is a long, continuous process. Soils in cool, dry climates tend to be shallower than those in warm, humid areas.

The texture and structure of a soil determine its amount of open space or pores. The amount of open space, in turn, determines how much water can percolate through the soil and the length of time water is retained in the soil. Sandy soil, for example, allows water to percolate rapidly through the soil, out of the reach of plant roots. A percolation test is given as an activity suggestion on page 25.

The texture of soil can be determined by rubbing a sample of the soil between damp finger and thumb.

- Sandy soil feels gritty.

- Silty soil feels smooth and slick or flour-like.

- Clay soil feels smooth, plastic, and very sticky.

A Soil Profile

Layers	0"
Organic material	2"
Topsoil	
	10"
Subsoil	
	30"
Parent material	
	48"

Source: Natural Resources Conservation Service.

These characteristics of soil allow different types of plants to grow in different areas. Some plants need particular nutrients, others tolerate growing in very wet soils, and some grow where there is very little organic matter in the soil. The roots of plants help to hold soil in place and therefore reduce erosion. A layer of organic matter such as dead leaves and grass on top of the soil also helps to reduce erosion and keep moisture in the soil during periods without rain.

If people continually walk in the same places, the soil becomes compacted and the ability of soil to absorb water is changed. If the roots of plants are damaged, they no longer help to hold the soil in place. It may look like great fun to run up the slope of a sand dune at the beach and roll back down, but doing so kills plants such as beach grasses that help to stabilize sand dunes so that the dune is not destroyed in a storm. The shortest way down a hill may be to hike straight down the slope, but if many people do this, the raindrops landing on this trail will follow the same path and a gully can quickly form that will erode the hillside. Trails that climb and descend

Soil erosion caused by soil compaction and overuse of a trail.

slopes are purposely laid out with S-shaped curves called switchbacks to reduce the possibility of erosion.

Soil eroded from the land is often deposited in a river, a lake, or, eventually, the ocean. These particles carried by the water smother the gills of fish and insects in the aquatic environment and eventually settle in quiet waters and smother creatures living there. Many outdoor recreation practices have been changed as we realize that we can and must reduce our negative impact on soil, water, and air quality in order for sites and opportunities to be available in the future.

Samples of soil particles of different sizes: sand, silt, and clay.

Recipe for an Ecosystem

Today your team will be exploring an ecosystem to find all the ingredients and how they are linked together. An ecosystem includes all the living things in an area and their environment.

Date: _____ Time: _____ Location: _____

Observers:

Environmental Conditions

Air temperature at ground level (take three readings):

_____

_____ Average _____

_____

Air temperature at chest height:

_____

_____ Average _____

_____

Orientation of site to sun _____

Wind speed _____

Wind direction _____

Relative humidity _____

Weather conditions _____

_____

% of overhead cover _____

Soil

Use a trowel to dig into the soil. Below, write in facts about the soil and draw a diagram to show the soil layers and their depths.

Color of soil _____

Odor of soil _____

Depth of soil_____

Temperature of soil _____

Texture of soil _____

Percolation test _____

Soil pH _____

Plants

Count the number of species of plants on the study site:

Upper level _____ Types _____

Middle level _____ Types _____

Ground level _____ Types _____

% of ground cover _____

Is there much variety of plants or a little? _____

Why? _____

How have these plants adapted for survival? _____

How have their seeds dispersed? _____

Animals

Survey the site for evidence of wildlife (homes, scat, pellets, tracks, nests, partially eaten food, chewed leaves, etc.). Record your findings:

Interactions

How do the environmental conditions affect the plants and animals in this ecosystem?

From the evidence you found, sketch the components of one food chain.

Name one animal you found and list three ways that its numbers might be limited by the other components of the ecosystem.

_____

_____

_____

Pick three words that best describe the ecosystem you studied:

_____   _____   _____

Looking at an Ecosystem

An ecosystem is the set of relationships between plants and animals and the nonliving parts of the environment such as soil, sunlight, water, and temperature. Ecosystems are complex and each component depends on the others and affects others. If a critical link in an ecosystem is destroyed, this may jeopardize the entire system. For example, a forest fire may kill a large stand of trees. Animals that depend on the trees for food and shelter are affected. The soil no longer receives vital nutrients from leaf decomposition. Plants that require shade will no longer grow. New populations of plants, birds, mammals, and insects which thrive in an open, unshaded area will slowly become established. The original forest ecosystem may be altered forever.

One way to help girls learn about the effects of weather and soils on plants and animals is to conduct an investigation of a particular ecosystem such as a meadow, desert, or forest and investigate the ingredients. The interaction of living organisms and nonliving factors is the recipe for the life and survival of an ecosystem. Copy and distribute the activity sheets on pages 134 and 135. Split girls up into teams to investigate the elements of the ecosystem and see what discoveries they make. They should be prepared to share their findings about the ingredients of the ecosystem which they plan to study.

Once girls have put together their observations and shared their findings, it will be easier for them to see and understand other ecosystems. They can observe the changes in ecosystems as they hike up a mountain or float down a river valley on a canoe trip.

Chapter 8

Planning for Trip Camping

Girl Scouts love to go on trips. Girls who enjoy camping can combine their camping skills with skills in hiking, biking, canoeing, horseback riding, or sailing, for example, to plan and carry out an exciting trip. They can visit state and national forests and parks, canoe down a scenic river, horseback ride or backpack into the backcountry, and have a wonderful time seeing new sights and testing their skills with their friends. These activities require time in planning and preparation, but the rewards are great. This chapter outlines the process for planning an extended camping trip and evaluating the experience afterwards.

8

In Girl Scouting, trip camping is defined as a camping experience planned and carried out by a group of girls who are experienced campers and their adult leaders. The group camps at different sites for three or more nights and travels from one site to another under its own power or by transportation that permits individual guidance of the vehicle or animal—for example, bicycle, canoe, horse, or sailboat.

Readiness

Here are some questions a leader might ask herself and her troop to determine if they are ready for trip camping.

Are the girls ready for trip camping?

Have the girls successfully planned and carried out several weekend camping trips?

Do they want to try more adventurous camping activities?

Can they work together as a team to perform daily living tasks such as meal preparation, setting up a campsite, and packing personal and group gear?

Do they have the skills for extended travel by the mode of transportation they want to use?

Are they willing to become physically fit enough to enjoy a trip where they are on the move?

Are they committed to the trip and do they have the time for the planning and trip preparation?

Do they have the basic skills in camping, first aid, food preparation, water purification, etc., for the particular type of trip?

Are they willing to earn the money needed for the trip?

Can they resolve problems that arise within the group?

Are the leaders ready?

If a troop wants to go trip camping, the troop leaders may not feel that they have all of the skills necessary to successfully carry out this type of trip. The leader can then help girls seek out persons in the council or community who can serve as consultants to the group or may choose to contract with a company to provide the services necessary for a raft trip or a horse packing trip, for example.

Review the following sections in *Safety-Wise*: "Planning Trips with Girl Scouts" (pages 126–140), the activity checkpoints on "Trip/Travel Camping" (pages 114–117), and the activity checkpoints

for the particular travel mode to be used (canoeing, horseback riding, etc.). Check the ratio of girls-to-adults needed for the trip. At least one of the adult leaders must be a female. Check with the local Girl Scout council for courses given on trip planning and other procedures related to trip planning that should be carried out through the various phases of the trip.

The persons leading the trip should possess the following skills or experiences:

- Trip planning with girls.

- Leadership of groups in outdoor settings.

- Assessment of the readiness of girls and the adults for the type of trip contemplated.

- Ability to plan progressive experiences to enhance group readiness.

- Safety management, including first aid and handling emergency situations.

- Minimal impact camping techniques.

- Program activities specific to the type of trip.

- Physical fitness and skills necessary to lead the group.

- Familiarity with the area in which the trip will be conducted.

- Ability to supervise and manage the group.

Planning and Preparation

Sound planning and teamwork are needed for a troop to go trip camping. The trip should be based on ongoing troop activities and interests. The trip must have a clear purpose that is formulated and understood by both girls and adults. The girls should have the ability to work successfully in groups, both large and small, and exhibit the maturity to accept the responsibilities the trip will bring. The adult leaders of the group must be willing to accept the responsibilities involved in carrying out the trip. Parents or guardians must support the plan, have confidence in the leadership, and be willing to support the girls.

Each girl should participate in the decision-making process about where the group will go and her goal in taking this type of trip. With the whole group, talk about the reasons to go on a trip, and the kinds of activities the girls would like to do on this trip. With an inexperienced group, the leader might give the girls a few suggestions and then let them start to develop their own list.

Brainstorming is a fun way to have the troop develop ideas for trip camping and places to visit. The girls can then do some research on these possibilities. They should discuss what information will be needed to make a group decision. Remind them that it is important to get as much information as possible about each destination and that this information will be used both to make the decision about which place to go and also later when more detailed planning is needed.

Once the information has been discussed with the whole group, it is time for the final decision to be made. Narrow down the choices to one. Remember that the trip should have a clear purpose formulated and understood by both girls and adults.

Once a trip destination and purpose have been established, it is time to fill in the details. Several months will be needed to plan and prepare for the trip.

The members of the group who are going on the trip can be divided into committees to work on portions of the plan. Each committee can work together to make a list of questions to ask as they search out information and plan the trip. Below are some questions that the committees might consider. Committee members will need to search out answers and be prepared to report back to the whole troop so that planning decisions can be made.

Program

What are the reasons for taking this trip?

Have any other groups we know gone to this place? What can we learn from them?

What activities are available during the day, in the evening, along the way?

When is a good time of the year to go?

What activities can be done while traveling?

Do we have the skills for this type of trip? How will we sharpen our skills?

Do we have the fitness necessary for this type of trip? How can we increase our fitness levels?

Safety

What prerequisite skills are needed by all girls and adults?

Will training be needed to get the group and adults ready?

How many adults are needed?

What permissions are needed?

What information is needed for the trip safety plan?

Is a first-aider needed? Is a lifeguard needed?

What are the contingency plans?

What code of behavior is needed for girls and adults?

8

Financing

How much will the trip cost?

Is additional insurance necessary?

How much of the troop treasury is budgeted for the trip?

Will the troop do special money-earning projects for the trip?

Is funding available from the Girl Scout council or other source?

Transportation

What types of transportation will be needed?

Who will provide the transportation?

How much time will be needed to travel from place to place?

Equipment

What equipment and clothing are needed?

Can equipment be rented at the site rather than carried?

What sources are available for borrowing or buying equipment and supplies?

Food

What arrangements will be necessary to feed the group? (Consider restaurants, picnics, cooking out.)

What will we eat? Where will we obtain food along the route? (Consider all religious, ethnic, medical, racial, and economic factors, and the needs of persons with disabilities, when planning menus and places to eat.)

Is it possible to keep perishable food cold while traveling and at stopovers?

Planning Checklist

Plan a realistic calendar that will allow time to complete the following items:

- Fill in the details of the itinerary and activities.

- Contact the Girl Scout council to obtain proper insurance for the trip.

- Plan the budget and carry out any needed money-earning projects.

- Hold pre-trip conditioning and skill-building sessions

- Design a safety management plan for the trip. Learn emergency evacuation and rescue procedures and what individuals should do if separated from the group. Know the council's plans for crisis management and when and how they should be used by the group.

- Make equipment lists for personal and group gear. Find the necessary equipment.

- Plan the procedures for developing menus, shopping, and packaging food.

- Discuss with girls a code of conduct for the trip and what is appropriate in different settings during the trip, such as when sharing campsites with other groups, meeting other parties on a trail, or being in public settings.

- Plan the details of transportation to and from the starting and ending points.

Practicing with the Mode of Transportation

Depending on the type of trip, a lot of practice may be needed for the particular type of transportation to be used. A bicycle trip, for example, requires that each girl's bike be adjusted to her size and checked to make sure that it is in good working condition. In addition to taking group bike trips of increasing lengths, each girl will need to ride frequently to keep in shape. She must learn how to pack her equipment appropriately to fit on the bike and practice with her bike fully loaded. The added weight means tougher pedaling and longer stopping distances when the brakes are applied. She should know how to make minor adjustments and repairs to her bike and equipment. She will need to review the rules of the road and how to ride safely with a group.

A canoe trip means a lot of practice in responding to the types of water conditions expected, in packing and loading gear, and in rescuing an overturned canoe and its occupants.

Working Together

In preparing girls for the trip camping experience, it is very important to bring the group together and help the girls learn to work as a team. Encourage the girls to work together in small groups to plan various aspects of the trip. Point out how this will help everyone to get the work done.

Some Girl Scout councils have challenge courses at their facilities that will provide the group with a fun-filled series of activities to develop teamwork. If such a facility is available, plan to use it as part of your preparation. Ask the facilitator to conduct activities that require teamwork.

Developing the girls into a team and getting them ready for a trip might include activities such as the one below. Exercises like these can help the leader measure the girls' maturity and can help the girls learn how to get along with each other during the trip. Each person in the group would be given a copy of this activity. Discuss with your group how these characteristics help people to work together.

The exercise on the next page can be used to find out how ready, willing, and able each person is to plan and make decisions in partnership with other girls and adults. Each person should be given a copy.

What Is Your M.Q. (Maturity Quotient)?

There are many characteristics of a person with the maturity to get along with others in a group setting. If an important one is not listed on the chart to the right, add your own ideas. Which of the following characteristics of a mature person do you possess?

Discuss with your group how these characteristics help people to work together.

Check all that apply to you.

_____ being open-minded

_____ being flexible

_____ not picking on small things

_____ sharing hard work

_____ being able to admit when you are wrong

_____ thinking before you speak

_____ knowing you are not perfect

_____ knowing other people are not always right

_____ respecting the rights of others

_____ being responsible

_____ being self-motivated

Working with Others

Put a dot (.) after each statement in the column that most closely represents your ability to work with other people (or your feeling about working with them).

I Am Ready	not really	somewhat	pretty much	very much
to trust others	____	____	____	____
to accept others	____	____	____	____
to be open	____	____	____	____
to be supportive	____	____	____	____
to try new ideas	____	____	____	____
to initiate change	____	____	____	____
to compromise	____	____	____	____
to share necessary information	____	____	____	____

I Am Able	not really	somewhat	pretty much	very much
to communicate clearly	____	____	____	____
to communicate honestly	____	____	____	____
to recognize prejudices	____	____	____	____
to take steps to overcome prejudices	____	____	____	____
to share my skills	____	____	____	____

I Am Willing	not really	somewhat	pretty much	very much
to treat others as unique individuals	____	____	____	____
to seek out their opinions	____	____	____	____
to understand their feelings	____	____	____	____
to seek out their reactions	____	____	____	____
to listen	____	____	____	____
to observe	____	____	____	____
to exchange opinions	____	____	____	____
to reserve judgment	____	____	____	____
to value the experience of others	____	____	____	____

Draw a line to connect the dots. In which columns do the dots tend to cluster?

The questionnaire on the previous page creates a profile of each person's partnership potential. The more that the dots are clustered toward the right side, the higher the girl's potential and the higher her M.Q. Discuss what the group members can do to become better at supporting each other and working together during their trip.

Support of Parents/Guardians

The support of parents/guardians is very important throughout the entire planning and preparation process. It is essential to keep parents/guardians informed at all times. In the beginning stages of planning, girls can help to develop an information sheet and take copies home to their families.

If the trip is an extended one or is unfamiliar to families, at least two meetings with the parents/guardians should be held before the trip. A preliminary meeting should be held several months before the expected departure date. This meeting should be

used to explain the purpose of the trip, costs, payment schedules, training sessions, specialty equipment, and clothing needs, as well as any special support the girls and leaders may need. Written materials such as a tentative trip itinerary, permission forms, photo releases, health history cards, health examination forms, and permission-to-treat forms can be handed out at this time. A month before the anticipated trip, the girls should plan another meeting of parents/guardians. Where possible, the girls should take the leadership of this meeting. The parents/guardians should be given copies of the final itinerary, codes of behavior for trip participants, equipment lists, a reminder of remaining payment dates, and the emergency contact list (see page 79). This meeting will give parents/guardians the opportunity to have any questions answered.

Final Preparation

The trip leader takes copies of all correspondence, reservation confirmations, receipts, canceled checks (or copies of checks), and other materials with her on the trip in case there is a problem with arrangements or reservations or if documentation of payment is needed. Before leaving, take the time to reconfirm all arrangements. This can be done by some of the girls with adult supervision. A girl/adult team handles the money and keeps records. A file containing all of the participants' health histories, permission forms to

participate, and insurance forms should accompany the group. Seal these in plastic bags to keep them secure during the trip. Make a final check concerning equipment, first aid kits, food, health of the participants, etc., and then enjoy the trip!

Evaluation

When the trip is over and the troop has returned home, evaluate the trip experience from start to finish. Discuss what was fun and worthwhile and what girls would like to change or eliminate on future trips. Find ways for the troop to build new activities based on their travel activities. Share experiences with others. Be sure to include parents/guardians in the evaluation process. These individuals can also provide insights to the troop. Topics to discuss after the trip might include the following:

Program

What activities did the group like best?

Which activities would the group like to do again?

Did the activity schedule work well? Was there too much or too little to do?

Was free time available?

Was the schedule flexible to allow for unexpected opportunities?

Did everyone have a job? Was there a fair distribution of work?

How effective was the code of behavior the troop established for this trip?

Which skills will the troop need to improve?

What did the girls learn?

What did the leaders learn?

What will they remember most about the trip?

Transportation

Did the arrangements for transportation work out well?

Was the group comfortable while traveling?

Was enough time planned for moving the group from one place to another?

Would the same travel provider/company be used again?

Was there enough personal space during the trip?

Was the traveling time just right or too much?

How did the activities planned during the traveling time work out?

What did the girls learn about living together under close conditions for a length of time?

Food

Were arrangements for feeding the group satisfactory?

Did the cooking equipment meet the needs of the menu?

Was the menu too complicated for the time allowed?

What would you change?

Did the group make any change to the menu or cooking methods during the trip and why?

Financing

Was the original budget effective?

If the budget was exceeded, how does the troop plan to take care of this?

If there is money left over, how will the group use this money?

What did the group learn about budgeting?

Equipment

Was all the equipment used? What else was needed?

How well did the group members choose personal gear?

Was enough training provided for the equipment used?

Leader Evaluation

The adults should ask themselves the following questions at the end of the trip:

- Did the adults work well together? Were supervision and other responsibilities shared among the adults?

- Were adults physically and emotionally prepared for this trip?

- Was there enough adult coverage, or would additional adults have been helpful?

- Were there any behavioral or medical problems that need further discussion or follow-up?

- If a problem occurred, could the situation have been handled in a better way? Was the council notified and a written report submitted?

A written record should be kept of the process of planning and evaluation for future trips. In addition, the girls may want to create a scrapbook or slide show of their experiences to share with families and other troops. It is time to celebrate their accomplishment!

Chapter 9

Camping in the Backcountry

Backcountry camping requires additional knowledge about how to minimize our impact and how to choose the proper equipment for the particular activity and the setting. This chapter reviews the principles of minimal impact camping for backcountry settings and the selection of equipment for trip camping.

Minimizing Impact*

As girls plan more advanced trips, they will need a more thorough understanding of minimal impact camping. The principles of minimal impact camping have been developed by federal agencies and by various organizations, such as the National Outdoor Leadership School, to

help people understand how they can reduce the impact of their outdoor activities on the environment. Many hundreds of people can camp and hike in the same areas each year if they are careful about their impact. Or an area may be devastated by the actions of just one person so that it must be closed to campers for many years until natural systems can repair the damage. Minimal impact camping (also called no-trace camping) requires personal responsibility and choosing the appropriate camping techniques for each situation. The following techniques are based on research conducted in the backcountry. Some of these techniques may change in the future as our understanding improves.

Plan Ahead and Prepare

Minimal impact camping requires advance planning as well as on-the-spot action. Establish a goal for the trip. Are the goal and activities desired by the group compatible with the location chosen for the trip? Before the trip, contact local authorities at the site of the planned expedition. Find out when the areas will be least crowded. Check to see if there is a restriction on the number of people in each group and if a permit is necessary for use of the area. Plan carefully for both activities and weather. Choose clothing and equipment in earth tones so that the colors blend in with the landscape.

Meal planning also requires advance preparation. Remember that appetites are generally bigger when girls are active in the outdoors. Plan for three meals each day and several snacks. If the trip is into the backcountry, be sure to take along extra food in case weather or some other emergency delays the group from reaching the final destination. Meals should be planned so that packaging and fuel requirements will be minimal. Before a backcountry trip, plan time at home to pretest the food for taste, texture, eye appeal, and quantity. If the package says "feeds two," check whether the volume is really enough to feed two ravenous hikers or whether it is too much. This is especially critical with some brands of freeze-dried foods.

* The main concepts in this section are based on the national Leave No Trace outdoor ethics program, as printed in the National Outdoor Leadership School's *Leave No Trace: Outdoor Skills and Ethics* series of 10 regional booklets, © 1995.

The amount spent on food can be adjusted according to the trip budget. Freeze-dried foods that are specially made for outdoor trips may weigh less than food bought at the grocery store, but often cost substantially more per serving. With creative menu planning and shopping, many of the foods needed can be found at the grocery store. A balance can be achieved by mixing and matching grocery store items with specialty backpacking food items that may have less weight and bulk. Foods such as margarine or peanut butter can go into squeeze tubes.

Generally food preparation is most efficient if the cooking group consists of two to four people. Dispersed, small groups can more easily minimize their impact on the environment. After purchasing the food, repackage it by meals and leave all cans, bottles, and boxes at home. Don't forget to enclose the cooking instructions with each meal. All the foods for each day can be packed together for each cooking group.

In the backcountry, especially in bear country, it is of vital importance to store food away from the tenting area. **Under no circumstances should any food be kept in a tent.** Food should be placed in a drawstring bag and hung on a rope between trees. In some national parks, hikers are provided with bear-proof

A wide variety of foods that will not spoil during a trip are available from grocery stores, from specialty camping stores, or by mail order.

containers for storing food. These containers have reduced the number of bear contacts with humans because the bears no longer associate people with food. Even in areas where bears are not a problem, if food is not stored properly, other animals can get into the food supply. If the food is ruined, the trip will most likely end prematurely. Consult with local authorities for recommended hanging or storage procedures.

Fire built on a flat rock.

Minimize the Use and Impact of Fires

The use of portable camping stoves is strongly suggested for trips. A one-burner stove is needed for each cooking group of two to four people. To reduce the need for fuel, plan nutritious meals that need little cooking time. Before departure, become well versed in the use of the campstove to be taken on the trip. If water is to be purified by boiling, be sure to carry additional fuel supplies.

If fires are allowed in pristine wilderness areas, the sites must be selected with utmost care to minimize the impact to the environment. Look for mineral soil, less than two to three inches of duff (decaying leaves and other matter), and areas away from trees, overhanging branches or rock ledges, grassy vegetation, and root systems. A small, shallow pit may be established by digging down to mineral soil or by looking for a spot with exposed sandy or mineral soil. Do not ring the area with rocks. Select a site away from trails or traffic patterns.

In areas where conditions make it unwise to build a fire pit, the flat rock method is an alternative (see above). Gather mineral soil from locations without vegetation. Spread several inches of mineral soil on top of a flat rock to keep it from becoming

blackened, and build the fire on top of the soil. Plan a fire just big enough to do the job so fuel will not be wasted. Make sure there is enough dead wood to sustain a fire. Walk at least 300 feet from the campsite to gather downed, dead wood. Collect only the wood needed.

Before leaving the site, restore any area where a fire pit has been built or a fire has been burned on a flat rock. If there are multiple fire pits, leave the most obvious, heavily used fire pit and dismantle the others.

Camp and Travel on Durable Surfaces

The concept of hiking comfortably and lightly on the land can be applied close to home or during wilderness travel. Even footsteps have an impact on the land. When traveling in an area with established trails, stay on the trails so that other areas will remain free of soil compaction. If the trail is designed to climb or descend a hill by curves and switchbacks, do not cut across country to save a few steps. This practice only disturbs more soil and vegetation and adds erosion and water runoff problems along the trail. Even when the trail is

Backcountry campsite.

muddy, resist the temptation to take a drier route. Stay on the trail rather than hiking along its edge to avoid starting a web of new trails. If the route is cross-country rather than on an established trail system, spread out rather than walk in line. There will be less likelihood of starting a new trail.

Use an established campsite whenever possible to concentrate the group's impact rather than disturb a new area. Studies on wilderness areas have shown that a group will degrade a well-used site less than if they start to use a new one. Most damage to a campsite occurs during its first few days of use. Use the well-worn trails to and from the site and set up tents and food preparation areas in locations that have already been disturbed.

If a well-established site cannot be located, find one that does not show signs of wear. If a new site must be chosen, disperse use and impact to the area. It is important to find a well-drained, level tent site. Avoid trampling fragile mountain meadows and areas close to the edge of a trail, stream, or lake. Although it is more convenient to camp near a water source, make camp at least 200 feet away from a body of water. Be sure to bring a collapsible container to transport water back to the campsite so that the group's activities will not take place near the water and pollute it. Find and use several routes to the water source rather than always taking the same path. If mosquitoes or flies present a problem, try to choose a site away from water. A breeze will help blow away flying insects.

When camping in a wooded area, look overhead for dead trees and hanging limbs that might fall in a windstorm. Decide which areas will be used for tenting, food preparation, and toilets. To minimize trampling of vegetation, choose areas that are far apart. Determine the direction of storm fronts and good weather fronts. Pitch tents for protection from storms by using the natural shelter provided by hills and vegetation. In summer, choose a site that will get sun in the morning and shade in the afternoon. Set up a cooking area that is sheltered from the wind.

Tents with waterproof floors make it unnecessary to dig a trench around a tent to divert rainfall, which only adds to the erosion of tent sites. If the group plans to stay at a site for more than two days, be careful that the vegetation does not become so trampled that it will not recover, particularly in areas with a short growing season. Wear soft-soled shoes and move to another site before your impact becomes noticeable.

Properly Dispose of What You Can't Pack Out

In the backcountry, cooking and cleanup are done in small groups. Dishwashing should be done at least 200 feet away from any water source. Scrape all food residue into a garbage bag. Wash the dishes, rinse them, and sterilize them in sanitizing solution or boiling water. Don't use untreated water to rinse the dishes! Since pots used in the backcountry are usually smaller than those at a troop campsite, dishes and utensils may have to be sanitized a few at a time. Air dry all cooking items by laying them out or hang them in a net bag. Scatter the dishwater at least 200 feet from any water source and your campsite. Remember, dirty water drained into a water supply can create a serious health hazard.

In a wilderness setting, if a latrine is not available, disposal of human waste must be done in a way to reduce the possibility of water pollution, to create conditions to speed decomposition, and to keep people and animals from discovering it. Ideally, urination should be done at least 200 feet away from any water source in an unvegetated area or on a large, flat rock.

Animals are attracted to the salt in urine. Urination in vegetated areas may cause animals to dig up soil and destroy plant life in order to eat the salty residue. The disposition of fecal matter is more complicated and depends upon the campsite, the geography, weather conditions, and the climate of the area. Campers along coastal regions, deserts, or rivers find a variety of solutions to deal with human waste. Check with local authorities to see if it is more environmentally sound to allow waste to decompose on the surface, bury it in a cat hole, or carry it out.

If the waste is to be buried, go at least 200 feet away from any water source, campsite, or trail. Use a trowel to dig a small hole about six inches deep into the organic layer of the soil. This is called a cat hole. After using the cat hole, mix the soil with the fecal matter, cover the hole, and hide it. Spread out the cat holes rather than locating them all in one area. Use a "pocket potty," a plastic bag, for used toilet paper, tampons, and sanitary napkins. Pack out the pocket potty.

If the group is winter camping, cover "yellow" snow. Because it is impossible to dig a cat hole in frozen ground, dig a cat hole in the snow. Since the fecal matter will be on the surface when the snow melts in the spring, try to select a site that will not be discovered by another camper.

As with dishwashing, all personal washing activities should take place at least 200 feet from the water source to reduce the potential of polluting it. To wash hands after going to the bathroom and before preparing food, use water from a water bottle, a small squeeze bottle of biodegradable soap, and a bandanna for drying.

In areas without showers, it is still important to keep clean. Sponge off with a bandanna or cloth dipped in warm water. When a more complete bath is needed, carry a container of water away from the water source, soap and scrub, and rinse off. Another, more luxurious option is to use a portable shower bag. Fill the bag and lay it out in the sun for several hours.

Portable shower bag.

The dark exterior of the bag will absorb the sun's rays. When the water is warm, hang the bag and take a shower.

In the backcountry, if clothes must be washed, try to use a minimum amount of soap. Soap can be difficult to rinse out, and the residue may irritate skin or the clothing may feel sticky. Hang clothes on a line strung away from other campers. Or, some hikers drape a few things over their packs to dry as they walk along.

Pack It In, Pack It Out

All disposable items, including food wrappings, food scraps, waste paper, toilet paper, and sanitary products, should be packed out from a backcountry campsite. Appropriate bags for disposal must be packed in. Take out trash left by previous campers, too, if possible. Keeping a campsite clean reduces problems with insects and small animals that are attracted to the smell of human food. Some soil conditions make decomposition in the soil a very slow process. Removing wastes from the campsite assures that animals will not dig up the sites searching for food scraps and reduces the signs of a group's presence for the next group to use the site. Make sure all cat holes are filled in and camouflaged. Before departing, take a careful look at the area to make sure that signs of the group's presence have been minimized.

Leave What You Find

For many people, camping in the backcountry is a special time to enjoy solitude and the unspoiled scenery. They do not want to hear, see, or camp near other groups. Whenever possible, pass by campsites already in use by others and locate a site elsewhere to minimize the impact of your group on the enjoyment of others. It is easier to be unseen if clothing, equipment, and tent colors blend in with the colors of the landscape. Leave radios and pets at home. Keeping the group small makes it easier to be quiet and enjoy the sounds of nature.

Before leaving, be sure to restore the vegetation—including moss, twigs, and pine cones—that might have been dug up for a fire pit or moved aside to pitch a tent.

Enjoy and leave behind the flowers, rocks, and artifacts found along the way so that others can have the same thrill of discovery. Take photographs, make sketches, or write a journal to preserve the memories of the trip.

Tips for Security at a Backcountry Site

- Notify authorities of the trip itinerary. Sign in at a ranger station or at a forest checkpoint. Check current weather and fire conditions and learn whether other campers have chosen the same destination.

- If vehicles will be left at the trailhead, find out if the parking area is patrolled. Unattended vehicles run the risk of vandalism.

- Beware of a littered campsite; this usually means the area is heavily used, which increases the chances of contact with strangers.

- Set up tents within sight of each other.

- Do not set up tents along major wildlife trails.

- Camp away from trailheads and trails.

- Report suspicious individuals to the person in charge.

- Be wary of individuals who ask too many questions, such as how many girls are on the trip, where are the girls from, how long are the girls staying, how many adults are with the group, etc.

- Be assertive, if necessary. Don't be afraid to ask an unwelcome visitor to leave the campsite.

- If traveling by canoes or bicycles, use chains and locks on equipment at night or when leaving the campsite unattended.

- Use the buddy system, as discussed on page 78.

Hiking Tips

- As a rule, backpackers can carry up to 20 percent of their weight. This may vary depending upon the length of the trip and the size and physical condition of the backpacker. To lighten her load, an individual who weighs 100 pounds or less may need to distribute some of her gear to others. A strong, fit person may easily carry more weight.

- For safety, each hiking group must have a minimum of four people. At least two adults must accompany every group. (If an injury occurs, one adult cares for the injured while the other adult and other person seek help.) Small groups usually have less impact on the environment.

- Hiking should be done during daylight hours. Plan your time well so that the group will have plenty of daylight remaining to set up camp.

- The hike should be manageable for everyone. Hikers can be grouped into small hiking groups by speed so that each group stays together. Let the slowest hiker set the pace at the front of the group. An adult should bring up the rear and make sure no one gets separated from the group.

- Allow time for rest stops, to eat, to drink, to readjust footgear, or to enjoy a scenic vista. Try to rest on a rock outcrop or unvegetated area whenever possible.

- Hikers should travel quietly or talk in low tones. If the group is noisy, the chances of seeing wildlife will be greatly reduced. Also, loud noises can bother other hikers.

Above all, take time to look, listen, and learn about the beauty of the area.

Hiking Shoes and Boots

Footwear for hiking ranges from sneakers and walking shoes, to lightweight boots with shallow lug soles made from a variety of synthetic materials, to heavy-duty leather boots with deep lug soles. Hiking boot and walking shoe selection should be done carefully while considering a number of factors:

- What will the terrain be like (flat, rocky, wet, muddy, off-trail, etc.)?

- How heavy a load will be carried?

- How much support do the hiker's feet and ankles require?

- Are the hiker's feet still growing?

- How much do the boots or shoes cost?

Sturdy walking shoes or lightweight hiking boots are usually adequate for light to moderate loads and on-trail hiking. Heavy boots are tiring to walk in and the lug soles tear up soil and fragile vegetation. Don't choose a pair of boots heavier than needed.

Fitting shoes and boots. Hiking shoes and boots should be purchased at a reputable outdoor equipment store. A trained salesperson can be very helpful in enabling you to narrow the choices. Look at the construction; shoes and boots should look well-made and sturdy. A poorly made boot may fall apart on the trail. Take the time to try on boots and walk around the store. Wear the sock combination to be worn with the boots.

Boots that don't fit in the store won't fit on the trail either. Boots should fit snugly but not constrict the feet. The heel should be seated firmly with no side-to-side and only a slight up-and-down motion. The toes should be about a finger's width from the front of the boot. The arch and ball of the foot should correspond to the shape of the boots. Lace the boots and walk around. If the boots don't feel right, try another pair.

Breaking in hiking boots. New hiking boots should be worn inside for the first few days to assure a comfortable fit. Boots that have been worn inside and show no signs of wear can often be exchanged. Before starting out on a long hike or backpacking trip, break in leather boots gradually. Over time, leather boots will mold to the hiker's feet. Boots made of synthetic material do not need a break-in period. Still, it is always wise to build up to longer hikes slowly to become more familiar with any pair of new hiking boots.

Foot Care

Proper foot care is very important. A painful blister can ruin a hike. On blistered feet, the weight of carrying a pack or portaging a canoe can be agony. In order to reduce the chances of getting blisters and to help absorb impact, many hikers wear two pairs of socks: wool or a wool/synthetic blend, or wool with an inner sock of cotton or synthetic material.

Some hikers change their socks several times during the day. Hikers should wash and dry their feet at the end of the day. Girls should not go to bed in sweaty socks. During the night, air should circulate around the feet. Girls should take enough socks for the trip or wash them out regularly.

During the first hour of any hike, it is a good idea to give everyone time to stop and readjust their shoes or boots and socks. At any time, if a hiker is experiencing rubbing or a "hot spot," she should ask the group to stop so she can place moleskin or molefoam padding around the site to halt further abrasions or pressure.

Tents

Tents should be chosen to suit the type of camping activity and to meet the shelter needs of the troop in the face of variables such as rain, snow, sun, wind, insects, and snakes. Consider the following questions during planning:

- How many girls are going on the trip and how many girls can share a tent?

- How much room is necessary for each person and her gear? Is it important to have standing room?

- How will the tents be transported, for example, by car to an established site, by backpack, horse, canoe, bicycle?

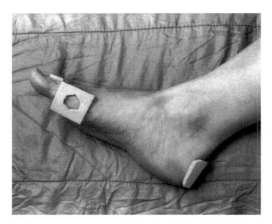

Moleskin or molefoam can be used to pad areas of pressure or abrasion.

- What styles of tents are needed? Dome? A-frame?

- What types of weather conditions are possible?

Other important features of a tent to consider are:

- Flame retardance.

- Weight.

- Capacity (both girls and equipment).

- Portability.

- Ease of setup.

- Ventilation.

- Floor design. (The floor should be constructed of durable materials and extend several inches up the side of the tent; the seams should be above ground to prevent leakage.)

- Number of doors and windows.

- Netting for insects.

- Waterproof material and design.

- Headroom.

- Waterproof tent fly.

- Pole construction (should be strong and lightweight).

- Strong zippers.

- Accessory interior pockets for small items and loops to hang a flashlight.

- Stakes and poles packed in a separate bag from the tent (to prevent holes in the tent).

- Fabric (breathable material to allow airflow).

- Color that blends with the environment.

Most tents are made of lightweight, fire-retardant materials, but no tent is fireproof. Never place a candle, camp stove, lantern, heater, open flame, or uncovered mirror in or near a tent. Pitch tents far enough from any cooking area so that the wind cannot blow a spark onto the tent. Never use plastic as a sleeping shelter because it is highly flammable.

Prior to the trip, check the condition of all the tents, poles, ropes, pegs, etc. Apply seam sealant to new tents as instructed by the tent manufacturer. Seam sealer can be obtained at a local sporting goods or hardware store. Apply several coats of sealant to the coated side of the tent fly and the seams of the tent, especially the floor seams. Allow the sealant to dry for 24 hours. This may be repeated as needed before future trips.

To extend the life of a tent, use a plastic sheet or ground cloth under the floor to give added protection from stones and sharp sticks and to keep the tent dry. Shoes should be removed before entering. Keep the interior clean by sweeping it out each day and shaking out the tent before packing it. To avoid making creases in the same places, it may be better to stuff a tent into its bag rather than fold and roll it. Make sure the tent is completely dry before storing it. Clean off the stakes and poles and place them in a separate bag. Materials to repair holes or rips in tents (needle and nylon thread, special tapes, or self-adhesive fabrics) and spare parts, including tent stakes, guy rope, and poles, should be included on all trips.

Pitching a Tent

Pitching a tent will be a manageable task at the campsite if the girls have practiced pitching the tent before the trip. To make the setup easier, assemble the matched poles and color code them with tape, paint, or permanent markers. Tents usually come with instructions for pitching. Remember to drive the tent stakes into the ground at a 90-degree angle to the guy rope (see next page). If camping in beach sand or on frozen soil, learn ways to anchor the tent in these conditions. Putting a plastic tarp under the floor and another on top of the floor of the tent will add protection from wetness. Make every effort not to disturb the environment. Do

Placement of tent stake.

including free-standing ones. An unstaked tent could blow over in a strong wind.

Storm Lashing

In case of high winds, use extra ropes and stakes, called "storm lashing," to secure a tent. Storm lashing helps prevent a tent from flapping, ripping, or being knocked down.

Depending upon the design, some imaginative storm lashing may have to be used to secure the tent. Some dome-shaped tents can be staked out using extra attachment points on the fly. If the fly completely covers the tent, run a rope from stake to stake by passing the rope under the fly and attaching the line to a tent pole, then back under the fly to another stake. Reverse the order using a second rope to form the double X shown.

not uproot large rocks or logs. Remove any loose stones, twigs, or branches from the ground, but leave pine needles and dead leaves as these will provide an extra cushion for sleeping. Stake out all tents,

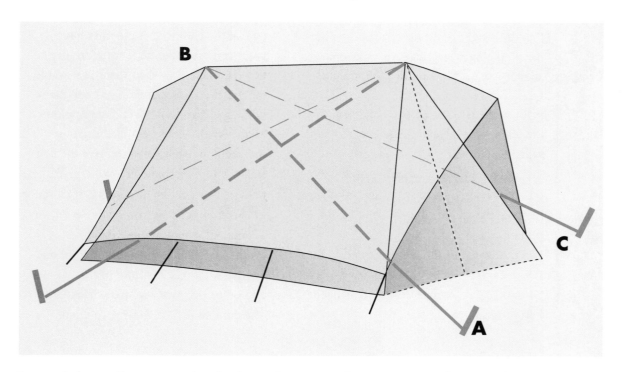

To storm lash a small tent, use two lengths of rope. Run one rope from its own tent stake A to and around the tent frame at B and back to peg C. Use the other rope in the reverse direction to form the double X shown. In this case the ropes are run between the fly and the tent.

Packs

The type of pack depends upon the requirements of the trip. There are three major styles of backpacks: frameless (day or fanny pack), internal frame, and external frame. A fanny pack is designed to be worn around the waist. Most fanny packs can hold a few small items. Fanny packs are best suited for around-town walks or short hikes. A day pack is a small pack designed to carry raingear, a lunch, a water bottle, a map, and a few extra items. Some people take a day pack on an extended backpacking trip in order to use it for day hikes during the trip. For comfort, a day pack should have padded shoulder straps. A girl who uses a wheelchair may carry a pack on the back of her chair. Do not overload her pack, but do recognize her ability to contribute to a hike.

Packs that are carried into the wilderness must be large enough to carry all necessities, including tents, sleeping bags, food, water, clothing, and emergency supplies. They must be rugged enough to stand the stresses of use. Packs are designed to accommodate different body sizes and shapes and must be fitted carefully. A poorly designed or improperly fitted pack will turn a wilderness adventure into an unpleasant experience.

Before choosing a type of pack, consider the following:

- Age and body size of the person.

- Type of trip (day hike or overnight).

- Amount of gear needed.

- Amount of weight the person can reasonably carry.

- Kind of activity that will take place—rock scrambling, ski touring, overnight backpacking.

- Ways to organize gear—all in one compartment, pockets, tied to the outside of the pack.

- Cost of the pack.

An internal frame pack fits close to the back and has a low center of gravity. It is best suited for activities such as rock climbing or cross-country ski touring where shifting weight can cause balance problems. An internal frame pack is preferable in dense, brushy terrain where an external frame pack would tend to get tangled in vegetation.

External Frame Pack

A quality external frame pack has a frame with a nylon pack, padded shoulder straps, and a padded hip belt. The pack usually has several compartments and pockets of varying sizes. The center of gravity is high, and by design the weight is transferred from the shoulders to the hips. An external frame pack is designed to support a heavy load. It is easy to pack and carry. Extra gear such as a sleeping bag or foam pad can be strapped to the frame. An external frame pack is best suited for travel on established trails.

Internal Frame Pack

Flexible reinforced supports, foam padding, and plastic sheeting give the internal frame pack the ability to conform to your body. This style of pack usually has two internal compartments, padded shoulder straps, a padded hip belt, and a network of buckles and straps used to adjust the fit. External pockets can be purchased separately and attached to the outside of the pack.

Where Do We Go Next?

Girls who enjoy camping have a world of opportunities waiting for them. Girl Scout leaders can help girls by alerting them to opportunities offered by the local Girl Scout council and at other sites across the nation.

Girls can start close to home by participating in vacation-time day camps sponsored by their Girl Scout council. Many councils also offer resident camps during the summer where girls from different troops sign up as individual campers and plan activities to take advantage of the opportunities that the site and staff can provide.

Girls can also use their skills to explore the world via the wider opportunities available through Girl Scouting. Each year Girl Scout councils across the country offer wider opportunities with nationwide participation. Cadette and Senior Girl Scouts throughout the country apply to attend these events. Although some do not require camping skills, others require previous camping experience in order to enjoy backpacking, bike hiking, canoeing, horsepacking, and rafting in backcountry areas from Florida to Alaska and Maine to Hawaii. There are international camporees, too, where girls can meet and camp with Girl Guides from around the world. Girls who return from these trips are eager to share their experiences with younger girls. Their stories help girls to understand the value of their membership and participation in Girl Scouting.

Appendix

Equipment for Overnight Trips

Choose items needed in accordance with requirements of trip, season, and activities.

Group Equipment	Basic	Advanced
Shelter		
__ tents (seam sealed, with fly, stakes, and all poles)		☐
__ extra stakes and guy ropes		☐
__ tent repair kit—including needle, nylon thread, and tape or adhesive fabric		☐
__ kitchen fly		☐
__ plastic ground cloths (to protect the floor of tent, or to cover gear)		☐
__ small dustpan and brush or sponge to clean tent		☐
__ thin foil blanket		☐
Cooking Equipment		
__ camp or backpack stove	☐	☐
__ stove repair kit	☐	☐
__ fuel	☐	☐
__ matches (wooden strike-anywhere type, in a waterproof container)	☐	☐
__ fire starters	☐	☐
__ pots and pans with lids	☐	☐
__ potholders or oven mitts	☐	☐
__ pot grips (auxiliary handles)	☐	☐
__ sharp knife, spatula, measuring cups (check menus)	☐	☐
__ long-handled spoon and fork (check menus)	☐	☐
__ can opener (check menus)	☐	☐
__ salt and pepper/spice kit	☐	☐

__ water jug/collapsible water container   ☐   ☐

__ cooler   ☐

__ food tubes   ☐

__ containers/plastic bags for leftover food   ☐   ☐

__ plastic garbage bags   ☐   ☐

__ large stuff sack and rope to hang food away from animals   ☐

Washing Supplies

__ biodegradable soap   ☐   ☐

__ dishpan (on lightweight trip, use other containers)   ☐

__ sponge or cloth   ☐   ☐

__ towel for drying pots   ☐   ☐

__ net bags for air-drying dishes and silverware   ☐   ☐

__ scouring pads   ☐   ☐

__ clothespins, rope for drying line   ☐   ☐

Group Tools/Supplies

__ licenses/permits   ☐   ☐

__ guidebooks   ☐

__ maps   ☐   ☐

__ flashlight   ☐   ☐

__ lantern, extra mantles or bulb and batteries   ☐   ☐

__ trowel   ☐

__ sharpening stone   ☐   ☐

__ first aid kit   ☐   ☐

___ external pack frame repair kit (toggles, clevis pins, split rings) ☐

___ sewing kit ☐ ☐

___ solar shower bag ☐

___ water filter/purification tablets (if needed) ☐ ☐

___ toilet paper ☐ ☐

___ small plastic bags ☐ ☐

Personal Equipment

Clothing

___ underwear ☐ ☐

___ long pants (cotton/wool) ☐ ☐

___ shorts ☐ ☐

___ T-shirts ☐ ☐

___ long-sleeved shirts ☐ ☐

___ sweaters and sweatshirts ☐ ☐

___ long underwear (top and bottom) ☐ ☐

___ socks ☐ ☐

___ bandannas ☐ ☐

___ sleepwear ☐ ☐

___ sturdy shoes/hiking boots ☐ ☐

___ sneakers/moccasins—for around tent site ☐ ☐

___ bathing suit ☐ ☐

___ sun hat ☐ ☐

___ wool hat ☐ ☐

___ gloves ☐ ☐

___ jacket ☐ ☐

___ water-repellent jacket, pants, and hat ☐ ☐

___ sewing kit ☐ ☐

Personal Hygiene Items

__ biodegradable soap and shampoo, towel, washcloth/bandanna, toothbrush, toothpaste, comb and brush, deodorant, sanitary napkins or tampons   ☐ ☐

__ sunscreen   ☐ ☐

__ lip balm   ☐ ☐

__ insect repellent   ☐ ☐

__ prescription medication (must be administered by an adult)   ☐ ☐

Sleeping and Eating Gear

__ sleeping bag/bedroll and plastic ground cloth   ☐ ☐

__ insulated ground pad   ☐

__ duffel bag or backpack   ☐ ☐

__ mess kit—plate, cup, bowl, eating utensils (wilderness campers often take only a cup and spoon)   ☐ ☐

__ water bottle   ☐ ☐

__ flashlight   ☐ ☐

__ extra batteries and bulb   ☐ ☐

__ nylon mesh bag for dishes   ☐ ☐

Program Items

__ compass   ☐ ☐

__ whistle   ☐ ☐

__ jackknife   ☐ ☐

__ work gloves   ☐

__ notebook and pencil   ☐ ☐

__ money   ☐ ☐

Glossary

Acute mountain sickness: A high-altitude illness that occurs when the body does not receive sufficient oxygen.

Backsighting: Looking back over the compass toward the point from which a person came to determine if she is on course.

Cat hole: A small hole dug about six inches deep into the organic layer of the soil for the purpose of burying fecal matter.

Cryptosporidium: A waterborne protozoan parasite that can be transmitted through person-to-person or animal-to-person contact or by ingestion of contaminated water or food. It causes diarrhea and is particularly harmful to persons who have compromised immune systems.

Day camping: Girls from different troops meet at an outdoor site each day for the duration of the session. They sign up as individual campers and are placed in temporary troops (units). The girls and troop leaders plan and carry out activities. Day camping is council-sponsored, and the council provides the staff, facilities, and site.

Declination: The angle between the direction in which the magnetic compass needle points and the true-north line; the difference in degrees between magnetic-north and the true-north in any given location.

Duff: Dead leaves, pine needles, twigs, etc., on top of the soil that are in the process of decaying.

Established site: A campsite that has been previously used. An established site may have latrines or flush toilets, picnic tables, a fire pit, etc.

First-aider: A person who has taken Girl Scout council approved first aid training. The level of first aid training is determined by the nature of the activity.

Frostbite: The freezing of body parts as a result of exposure to extremely low temperatures.

Fuel: Anything that supplies energy to a fire, such as wood, propane, butane, gasoline, or charcoal. Specifically in fire building, the term fuel is used to describe large pieces of wood that keep a fire going after it has been started.

Giardia lamblia: A protozoan found in many natural surface-water sources that can cause diarrhea, nausea, loss of appetite, cramps, weakness, vomiting, and dehydration if ingested.

Girl Scout camping: An experience that provides a creative, educational opportunity in group living in the outdoors. Its purpose is to utilize Girl Scout program, trained leadership, and the resources of the natural surroundings to contribute to each camper's mental, physical, social, and spiritual growth.

Heat exhaustion: The body's reaction to dehydration and prolonged exposure to high temperatures. Symptoms include headache, nausea, vomiting, and possible fainting.

Heatstroke: A life-threatening condition characterized by an extremely high body temperature and disturbance of the sweating mechanism.

Hypothermia (lowered body temperature): A potentially life-threatening situation in which the body loses heat faster than it can produce it. Wind, moisture, and cool temperatures can draw heat away from the body at a rapid rate.

Itinerary: The planned route to be followed on a journey or trip (includes places, dates, lengths of stay).

Kaper chart: A chart that lists the jobs that need to be done and the people who will do them.

Layering: Dressing for the outdoors by wearing a number of loose-fitting garments rather than one or two heavy garments.

Lyme disease: A bacterial infection that is transmitted by the bite of an infected tick. If the infection is left untreated, arthritic-like symptoms as well as heart and nervous system complications can occur.

Mineral soil: Soil that does not contain organic material.

Minimal impact camping (low-impact camping): A method of outdoor living that encourages each person to camp lightly on the land and leave no trace of her presence. The physical landscape of the campsite is preserved as well as the solitude and spirit of the wilderness.

Outdoor education: Effective utilization of Girl Scout program in the outdoor setting, enabling girls to grow in each of the areas of the four Girl Scout program goals. The primary approach is experiential learning through which girls develop their outdoor recreational interests and skills.

Orienteering: The use of map and compass to navigate a course.

Packing out: Removal of all trash and other discardable materials from a site.

Personal Flotation Device (PFD): A life preserver, buoyant vest, ring buoy, buoyant cushion, or special-purpose water safety buoyant device designed to keep a person afloat in the water.

Pocket potty: A plastic bag used to pack out used toilet paper, tampons, and sanitary napkins.

Priming: Making a backpack stove ready for use by raising the temperature of liquid fuel so that some of it vaporizes and lights. This is done according to the manufacturer's instructions. It is needed on some types of stoves.

Resident camping: A camping experience in which the campers take up residence for five days (120 hours) or more at an established site. Girls from different troops/groups sign up as individual campers and are placed in temporary units. The girls and their counselors plan activities, taking advantage of the opportunities available to them. Resident camping is council-sponsored and operated, and the council provides the total staff, facility, and site.

Scat: Fecal matter or droppings from an animal such as a fox, raccoon, or mouse.

Storm lashing: Crossed roping over the outside of a tent, or between the tent and the fly, that is designed to hold the tent in place in very windy conditions.

Trailhead: The place where a trail begins.

Travel camping: A camping experience planned and carried out by a group of experienced participants and their leaders or staff. The group uses motorized transportation to move from one site to another over a period of three or more nights. Travel campers use camping sites as a means of accommodation. Motorized transportation is normally a bus, van, or automobile, but it may be an airplane, a houseboat, a train, or a combination of these.

Trip camping: A camping experience planned and carried out by a group of girls who are experienced campers and their adult leaders. The group camps at different sites for three or more nights and travels from one site to another under its own power or by transportation that permits individual guidance of the vehicle or animal—for example, bicycle, canoe, horse, or sailboat.

Troop/group camping: A camping experience of 24 or more consecutive hours, planned and carried out by a troop/group of Girl Scouts and troop/group leaders, using sites approved by the council.

Bibliography

Girl Scout Resources

Cadette and Senior Girl Scout Interest Projects. 1987. Cat. No. 20-792.

Cadette Girl Scout Handbook. 1995. Cat. No. 20-916.

Caring and Coping: Facing Family Crises. Contemporary Issues Series. 1988. Cat. No. 26-825.

Ceremonies in Girl Scouting. 1990. Cat. No. 26-801.

Developing Health and Fitness: Be Your Best! Contemporary Issues Series. 1992. Cat. No. 26-833.

Earth Matters: A Challenge for Environmental Action. Contemporary Issues Series. 1990. Cat. No. 26-827.

Exploring Wildlife Communities with Children, by Carolyn L. Kennedy. 1981. Cat. No. 19-985.

Focus on Ability: Serving Girls with Special Needs. 1990. Cat. No. 26-800.

From Backyard to Backcountry: Camping Lightly on the Land (15-min. slide show). 1991. Cat. No. 13-760.

Games for Girl Scouts. 1990. Cat. No. 20-902.

Girl Scout Badges and Signs. 1994. Cat. No. 20-914.

Girls Are Great: Growing Up Female. Contemporary Issues Series. 1987. Cat. No. 26-822.

The Guide for Junior Girl Scout Leaders. 1994. Cat. No. 20-913.

Into the World of Today and Tomorrow: Leading Girls to Mathematics, Science, and Technology. Contemporary Issues Series. 1987. Cat. No. 26-823.

Junior Girl Scout Handbook. 1994. Cat. No. 20-912.

Reaching Out: Preventing Youth Suicide. Contemporary Issues Series. 1987. Cat. No. 26-824.

A Resource Book for Senior Girl Scouts. 1995. Cat. No. 20-917.

Safety-Wise. 1993. Cat. No. 26-201.

Staying Safe: Preventing Child Abuse. Contemporary Issues Series. 1986. Cat. No. 26-82.

Valuing Differences: Promoting Pluralism. Contemporary Issues Series. 1990. Cat. No. 26-828.

Other Resources

Camping

Barker, Harriet. *Supermarket Backpacker.* Chicago: Contemporary Books, 1977.

Bouwman, Fred, et al. "Just Say 'No' to Untreated Water." *Backpacker,* June 1992, pp. 51–59.

Brown, Tom. *Tom Brown's Field Guide to Nature and Survival for Children.* New York: Berkley Publishers, 1989.

Fleming, June. *The Well-Fed Backpacker.* New York: Vintage Books, Random House, 1986.

Getchell, Dave. "Safe Havens." *Backpacker,* April 1992, pp. 19–25 (article on tents).

Gorman, Stephen. "Pedestrian Pleasures." *Backpacker,* April 1992, pp. 87–90 (article on hiking boots).

Hampton, Bruce, and David Cole. *Soft Paths: How to Enjoy the Wilderness Without Harming It.* Harrisburg, Pa.: Stackpole Books, 1988.

Harmon, Will. *Wild Country Companion.* Helena, Mont.: Falcon Press Publishing, 1994.

Hodgson, Michael. *Wilderness with Children: A Parent's Guide to Fun Family Outings.* Harrisburg, Pa.: Stackpole Books, 1992.

Howe, Steve. "Portable Infernos." *Backpacker,* April 1992, pp. 78–82 (article on backpack stoves).

Jenkins, Mark. "Pack Sense." *Backpacker,* April 1992, pp. 53–57.

Kahn, Hal, and Rick Greenspan. *The Camper's Companion: The Pack-Along Guide for Better Outdoor Trips.* San Francisco, Calif.: Foghorn Press, 1991.

Manning, Harvey. *Backpacking, One Step at a Time.* New York: Vintage Books, Random House, 1986.

McHugh, Gretchen. *The Hungry Hiker's Book of Good Cooking.* New York: Alfred A. Knopf, 1982.

National Outdoor Leadership School. *Soft Paths.* 1990 (15-min. videotape). P.O. Box 18, Lander, Wyo. 82520.

Rennicke, Jeff. "Sweet Dreams." *Backpacker,* April 1992, pp. 33–40 (article on sleeping bags).

Ross, Cindy. *Hiking*. New York: Fodor's Travel Publications, 1992.

Simer, Peter, and John Sullivan. *The National Outdoor Leadership School's Official Wilderness Guide*. New York: Simon & Schuster, 1983.

Wiltsie, Meredith. "Most Excellent Kids' Camping Gear." *Outside,* August 1992, pp. 115–118.

Wirth, Bob. *Backpacking in the Eighties*. West Nyack, N.Y.: Parker Publishing Company, 1983.

Knots

Cassidy, John. *The Klutz Book of Knots*. Palo Alto, Calif.: Klutz Press, 1985.

Owen, Peter. *The Book of Outdoor Knots*. New York: Lyons & Burford, 1993.

Environmental Activities

Cornell, Joseph. *Sharing the Joy of Nature: Activities for All Ages*. Nevada City, Calif.: Dawn Publications, 1989.

The Earthworks Group. *50 Simple Things Kids Can Do to Save the Earth*. Kansas City, Mo.: Andrews and McMeel, 1990.

Harris, Mark D. *Embracing the Earth*. Chicago, Ill.: The Noble Press, 1990.

National Wildlife Federation. *Wild About Weather*. Ranger Rick's NatureScope series. Washington, D.C.: NWF, 1991.

Health and Safety

American National Red Cross. *First Aid: Responding to Emergencies*. St. Louis, Mo.: Mosby—Year Book, 1991.

Johnson, Becca Cowan. *For Their Sake: Recognizing, Responding to, and Reporting Child Abuse*. Martinsville, Ind.: American Camping Association, 1992.

National Safety Council. *First Aid and CPR, Level 2*. Boston: Jones and Bartlett Publishers, 1991.

National Safety Council. *First Aid and CPR, Level 3*. Boston: Jones and Bartlett Publishers, 1991.

National Safety Council. *First Aid Essentials*. Boston: Jones and Bartlett Publishers, 1988.

Vogel, Stephen, and David Manhoff. *Emergency Medical Treatment: Children*. Wilmette, Ill.: EMT Inc., 1989.

Orienteering

Disley, John. *Your Way with Map and Compass—Orienteering.* Willowdale, Ontario: Canadian Orienteering Service, 1973.

Kals, W. S. *Land Navigation Handbook: The Sierra Club Guide to Map and Compass.* San Francisco, Calif.: Sierra Club Books, 1983.

Kjellstrom, Bjorn. *Be Expert with Map and Compass: The Orienteering Handbook.* New York: Macmillan, 1976.

Lowry, Ron, and Ken Sidney. *Orienteering Skills and Strategies.* Willowdale, Ontario: Orienteering Ontario, 1985.

McNeill, Carol, Jean Ramsden, and Tom Renfrew. *Teaching Orienteering.* Perthshire, England: Harveys, 1987.

Trips by Water

Bechdel, Les, and Slim Ray. *River Rescue.* 2nd ed. Boston, Mass.: Appalachian Mountain Club Books, 1989.

Kuhne, Cecil. *Advanced River Rafting.* Mountain View, Calif.: Anderson World, 1980.

Stories of Women in the Outdoors

Blum, Arlene. *Annapurna: A Woman's Place.* San Francisco, Calif.: Sierra Club Books, 1980.

LaBastille, Anne. *Women and Wilderness.* San Francisco, Calif.: Sierra Club Books, 1984.

Children's Stories

Baylor, Byrd. *Everybody Needs a Rock.* New York: Macmillan, 1985.

Curtis, Chara M., and Cynthia Aldrich. *All I See Is Part of Me.* Bellingham, Wash.: Illumination Arts Publishing Company, 1989.

Frasier, Debra. *On the Day You Were Born.* Allyn Johnston, ed. New York: Harcourt Brace Jovanovich, 1991.

Luenn, Nancy. *Mother Earth.* New York: Macmillan, 1992.

O'Connor, Jane. *Amy's (Not So) Great Camp-out.* New York: Grosset & Dunlap, Inc., 1993.

Seuss, Dr. *The Lorax.* New York: Random House, 1971.

Waber, Bernard. *Ira Sleeps Over.* Boston, Mass.: Houghton Mifflin, 1987.

Williams, Vera B. *Three Days on a River in a Red Canoe.* New York: Greenwillow, 1981.

Wirth, Victoria. *Whisper from the Woods.* New York: Simon & Schuster, 1991.

Index

Notes

Learning About the Environment